»THE SECRETS TO«
GREAT CHARCOAL GRILLING
»ON THE WEBER«

MORE THAN 60 RECIPES TO GET DELICIOUS RESULTS FROM YOUR GRILL EVERY TIME

BILL GILLESPIE

Bestselling author of *Secrets to Smoking on the Weber Smokey Mountain Cooker and Other Smokers* and *The Smoking Bacon & Hog Cookbook*

WITH TIM O'KEEFE

PAGE STREET
PUBLISHING CO.

PAGE STREET
PUBLISHING CO.

Copyright © 2018 Bill Gillespie

First published in 2018 by
Page Street Publishing Co.
27 Congress Street, Suite 105
Salem, MA 01970
www.pagestreetpublishing.com

Distributed by Macmillan, sales in Canada by The Canadian Manda Group.

22 21 20 19 18   1 2 3 4 5

ISBN-13: 978-1-62414-506-3
ISBN-10: 1-62414-506-X

Library of Congress Control Number: 2017952232

Cover and book design by Page Street Publishing Co.
Photography by Ken Goodman

Printed and bound in China

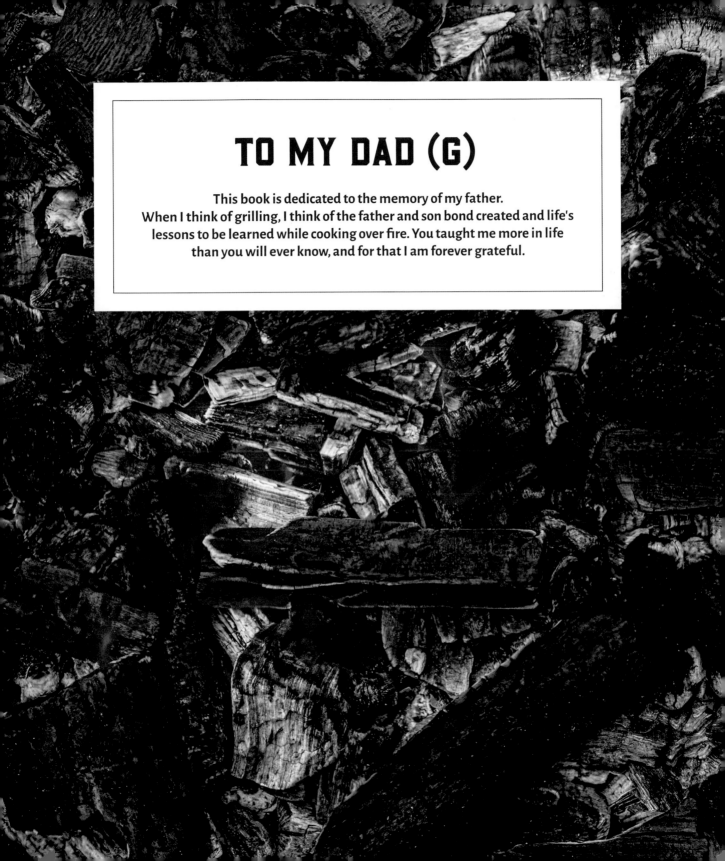

TO MY DAD (G)

This book is dedicated to the memory of my father.
When I think of grilling, I think of the father and son bond created and life's
lessons to be learned while cooking over fire. You taught me more in life
than you will ever know, and for that I am forever grateful.

CONTENTS

FOREWORD
BY LUKE DARNELL,
BARBECUE WORLD CHAMPION

Grilling and barbecue are an American art form, second only to the blues. We spend countless hours with many different tools creating spectacular dishes out of meat, fire and fun for our friends, family and loved ones.

Family and loved ones. They are the reason that we spend these hours learning and refining our craft. To bring smiles to their faces and contentment to their stomachs.

Smiles are present wherever Bill Gillespie goes. From having beers on Friday nights after preparations for a barbecue contest to the ever-present laugh, smile and "POW!" at the awards ceremony, Bill is as consistent as his cooking.

I've had the pleasure of cooking against Bill many times and also with him. We first met in 2014 when Bill won the American Royal Invitational. We've been the best of friends since. One thing is for certain—Bill loves cooking outside. This passion and joy shows in everything he does, from his cookbooks to his barbecue sauce.

The recipes in this book were designed with ingredients that you can find in any grocery store, simple to prepare and guaranteed to wow your company.

The best things about grilling and Bill's recipes are that there are no screwups or mistakes that aren't still going to be tasty!

So do yourself a favor—take this book to the grocery store, buy the ingredients for a couple of recipes, crack a cold one and get grilling! You'll be saying, "POW."

INTRODUCTION

Glowing red embers and warm summer nights. One of my favorite things about cooking on a grill is the smell of burning charcoal. It immediately brings me back to my childhood. Through thick wisps of smoke, I can practically see my father standing next to the grill, even though it's been almost ten years since his passing. For me, it's part of what makes cooking in the backyard magical.

My ride in the world of competition barbecue has been filled by many long hours driving to contests, years of experimenting to understand what judges prefer, numerous laughs with friends, along with my share of successes and failures. It's been said that within victory lies defeat, and within defeat lies victory. In many ways, I think my greatest victory also harbored defeat.

I still remember driving to the Jack Daniel's World Championship Invitational Barbecue Contest back in 2011. My hands gripped the steering wheel of a quad cab pickup truck, as I traveled over 1,100 miles to the most prestigious contest in competition barbecue. In the early dawn hours, driving through Ohio with my teammates asleep in the truck, I spotted a tractor trailer for Panther Premium Logistics. The logo on the side of the truck reminded me of a tattoo my father had on his forearm. I sat in the quiet and smiled, just listening to the hum of the road beneath the vehicle. I had never heard of that company, but I took it as a sign of good luck, because I knew my father was with me in spirit.

That year, I was fortunate enough to hear the judges call my name for first place overall—POW! Just like that, I somehow won the Jack! It was a great experience, and it took some time for all of it to sink in. Like lots of other people, my earliest memories of backyard cooking involved my father, but my father wasn't able to participate in the victory celebration. A few years later, while retelling this story, the idea for this book began to form in my mind. This book is inspired by memories of cooking with my father, and its purpose is to help people who want to become better backyard cooks.

Food brings people together, and it's usually part of family traditions that create memories. What better way to create family memories than with traditional Southern barbecue? Authentic barbecue requires a low-and-slow cooking method, which takes hours and hours. That means there's a whole lotta time people can spend together waiting for that delicious food to be served!

This book provides insights about your Weber kettle grill. Many people have told me they prefer to cook on a gas grill. The most common explanation is that it's quick and easy. I believe them. I have to believe them. And the reason I have to believe them is that I haven't cooked on a gas grill in so many years that I don't even remember how to light those things. No matter how simple a gas grill might be to use, simplicity cannot replicate authenticity. For me, a gas grill simply can't provide the same flavor as cooking over charcoal. It doesn't even come close!

Weber kettle grills are extremely versatile. If you learn some basic culinary skills, along with just two cooking methods, you'll discover an endless variety of dishes you can create. Pretty soon, you'll be enjoying perfectly cooked, moist, juicy burgers time and time again. But that's just the beginning. We'll also discuss a few different methods for preparing steak, including searing it directly on the hot charcoal! Later in this book, we'll even discuss how to configure your Weber kettle so you can make pizza. As you become a better backyard cook, you'll learn you can adapt techniques and mix ideas from different recipes.

A lot of people say that charcoal takes too long but it only takes 15 or 20 minutes to start the fire using a charcoal chimney. So that usually provides sufficient prep time. There are numerous dishes you can cook on a charcoal grill in 30 to 60 minutes. If you're willing to learn a handful of basics, you'll be able to cook just about anything you want, and you'll be able to do it right in your own backyard. Still doubt it? Stick with me, work your way through these chapters, and I think you'll begin to look at things a little differently.

Bill Gillespie

ALL UP IN YOUR GRILL

Congratulations on taking your first step on a new adventure in backyard grilling! While I'm not a chef by training, I've had a lot of success at grilling and barbecue contests. As a kid, I used to like to dunk my McDonald's french fries into my strawberry milk shake. If I can go from that to winning the two biggest contests on the competition barbecue circuit, then I think I can help you become a better backyard cook. This chapter contains information about your Weber kettle grill, basic culinary techniques, smoke woods and some tips and best practices. In this chapter, you'll learn about two basic cooking techniques: direct and indirect. If you master these two techniques, you can cook almost anything.

I realize a lot people reading this book might not necessarily be interested in the information pertaining to competition barbecue. The competition barbecue chapter essentially takes what I do at a contest and breaks it down into a process you can use on your Weber kettle grill. Before we get to that, I really want to make sure you develop an understanding of the various ways you can configure the Weber kettle. Understanding the different cooking configurations is a key part of becoming a better backyard cook. Enough of the talk, let's get down to business!

SETTING UP YOUR GRILL

The Weber kettle is made up of three sections: the stand, the base and the lid. It's pretty much a porcelain-enameled metal sphere on a tripod that is easy to clean and highly resistant to corrosion.

At the bottom of the base, there is one three-hole vent. The interior of the base contains a heavy, premium-gauge metal grate the holds the hot charcoal. The amount of oxygen that flows through the vent and reaches the charcoal ultimately determines cooking temperature. As more oxygen reaches the hot charcoal, the temperature increases. The interior of the base also contains the cooking grate where raw, uncooked food gets turned into something delicious.

The lid securely fits atop the base and contains one air vent. This vent typically remains fully open and is crucial for channeling air and smoke through the grill. Airflow into the grill sustains the heat source. If you completely close the top vent, airflow through the grill is severely limited, and the hot charcoal will slowly burn out. The lid is a spherical shape that reflects heat back toward the cooking grate, an important concept to understand.

I'm not endorsed by Weber, but I think their products are outstanding. The thing I like most about the Weber kettle is the versatility it provides. It's quick to set up, easy to use and simple to transport. It's also easy to configure in different ways, in order to take advantage of a variety of cooking methods. Some people might think Weber kettle grills are a little pricey. To me, for what you're getting, it's worth the $150.

HOW A CHARCOAL GRILL WORKS (SCIENCE STUFF)

Some people like to get into the superscience of backyard cooking. Not me; I like to keep it simple. For me, cooking comes down to flavoring food, controlling temperature and transferring heat. In the Weber kettle, charcoal acts as a fuel source that generates heat. The heat spreads in three ways: conduction, convection and radiation. The way I like to explain it goes something like this:

- Conduction is the transfer of heat by direct contact, such as placing raw food directly onto a hot cooking grate. Essentially, heat travels from the hotter object to the colder one by way of physical contact.

- Convection is the transfer of heat by air molecules, such as the airflow channeling within the kettle.

- Radiation is the transfer of thermal energy without direct contact, such as the heat bouncing off the lid and reflecting back toward the cooking grate.

When you cook on the Weber kettle, you're utilizing all three methods to transfer heat from the hot charcoal to the food. Essentially, you're bringing heat to the outermost surface of the food, and when the food's surface heats up, it then conducts heat inward toward its center. That's basically all there is to it. Not so bad for science stuff, right?

As a chef, the challenge of cooking is not only knowing the best way to transfer heat to different foods—the challenge is also being able to identify when food is properly cooked, so you know when to remove it from the grill. In the end, what you really need to understand is that there are two primary cooking methods you'll use in different ways: direct cooking and indirect cooking. The versatility of the Weber kettle allows you to take advantage of both methods, and we'll discuss them in just a little bit.

Single layer of charcoal covering the bottom of the grill.

CHARCOAL AND FIRE

One of the things many people enjoy about cooking in the backyard is that they get to play with fire! When cooking on a Weber grill, charcoal acts as the fuel source that creates heat. You have two types of charcoal to choose from: lump charcoal or charcoal briquettes.

Lump charcoal is essentially burnt wood, sold in bags. There are several brands of lump on the market. A lot of people consider lump charcoal to be a cleaner fuel source than charcoal briquettes. Lump charcoal typically burns a little hotter than briquettes, but it has a shorter burn duration. Typically, bags of lump charcoal contain chunks of varying sizes, which produces slightly inconsistent burn times.

Most backyard cooks are already familiar with charcoal briquettes. Essentially, briquettes are made from lump charcoal that is pressed into squares. As a result, briquettes contain binding agents to help them retain their shape. Some people prefer to light charcoal briquettes and let them turn gray before cooking on them. This helps prevent the chemicals that act as binding agents from adversely flavoring food. Several manufacturers sell what are called natural briquettes. These products tend to use natural binding agents, such as corn starch, to help the bricks retain their shape. One advantage to cooking with briquettes is that their uniform shape helps provide a more consistent burn time. As a general rule, I prefer to cook with natural briquettes.

Some backyard cooks like to use the same type of charcoal each and every time they prepare food. This is a good idea, particularly as you're learning to cook on your Weber kettle. Not only will you become familiar with the burn time the specific charcoal brand provides, you'll also get better at estimating how long foods need to cook. When I cook in the backyard, I prefer to use a charcoal chimney to light the charcoal. A charcoal chimney is easy to use. You simply create a small fire at the base of the chimney, and in about fifteen minutes the charcoal is ready to use. To get the fire going, you can light a piece of crumpled up newspaper, a few paper towels drizzled in olive oil or any camp fire starter tab available from a variety of manufacturers. When you see fire shooting up above the charcoal at the top of the chimney, that's usually a good sign the charcoal is hot and ready to use. I never use charcoal lighter fluid to initiate the fire, because I think the fluid infuses a nasty flavor into the food I'm cooking.

DIRECT COOKING

Direct cooking is what most people think of when it comes to backyard cooking. You like grilling burgers and dogs, right? This is a form of high-heat cooking, where food is placed directly over red-hot charcoal. Direct cooking generally works well for thin cuts of meat and similar proteins. One advantage of this method is that food cooks quickly. It's a preferred way to cook lean meats, as they'll be less likely to dry out.

Configuring your grill for direct cooking is ridiculously simple. Just light up a charcoal chimney, and when the edges of the charcoal at the top of the chimney start to turn gray, dump the hot coals into your grill. Using metal tongs, form an even layer of charcoal to help eliminate hot spots and create a uniform cooking environment. Direct cooking works well for the following food items:

Loaded charcoal chimney.

Burgers	Lobster
Chops	Vegetables
Drumsticks	Fish
Shrimp	Lamb
Steaks	Venison
Scallops	Bison

Ideally, you want the cooking grate about six inches/15 cm above the heat source. When I use the direct cooking method, I usually try to fill the bottom of the grill about two-thirds full. This is more than enough fuel to cook various foods. You should get 50 to 60 minutes of burn time from one chimney of lit charcoal.

Something to keep in mind about this cooking method is that it is prone to annoying flare-ups. A common source of flare-ups is fat drippings. Although these drippings can smolder and create smoke that helps flavor food, the shooting flames can become unwieldy. One way to help prevent flare-ups is to keep the lid on the grill. Another way, and the way I prefer, is to use a different cooking method for fatty meats.

INDIRECT COOKING

When you configure the grill for this method, the food you are cooking is not directly above the heat source. This cooking method is less prone to flare-ups and creates an enhanced flavor in food, particularly if you cook using smoke wood. There are actually two different ways to configure your Weber kettle grill for indirect cooking. One way enables you to cook using indirect heat at a high temperature. This method is great if you're cooking large, lean proteins, such as a beef rib-eye roast, pork loin, a whole turkey or whole chicken. The other way enables you to cook with indirect heat at a low temperature for a long period of time. This is the best method I've learned for making traditional Southern barbecue right on your Weber grill. While it takes a little time to get used to each of these methods, believe me when I tell you they're certainly worth learning!

High-Heat Roasting, Indirect (The Devil's Den)

Use the high-heat indirect method to cook at temperatures around 320°F to 350°F/160°C to 177°C. It's easy to maintain and will produce excellent results for various roasts, whole turkeys or whole chickens. To use this method, simply fire up 54 briquettes in a charcoal chimney. As soon as the bricks at the top of the chimney start to turn gray, dump the chimney into the grill. Using metal tongs, form the hot coals into two piles, on each side of the grill, with 27 bricks in each pile. Make sure the center of the grill contains no hot charcoal. Adjust the vents so the bottom vent is halfway open and the top vent is fully open. Every 35 to 40 minutes, add 8 unlit bricks to each pile of hot charcoal.

This method works well for the following items:

- Whole turkeys
- Whole chickens
- Pork loin
- Beef rib eye
- Roasts

A grill set up with charcoal baskets.

A grill set up with firebricks.

WEBER SELLS A HINGED COOKING GRATE. which makes adding charcoal to the fire a little easier. If you don't have a hinged grate, you can still use this cooking method, just make sure to align the handles on the cooking grate directly over the piles of hot charcoal so that you can insert additional bricks, as needed. This cooking method is easier if you have the hinged grate and the metal charcoal baskets.

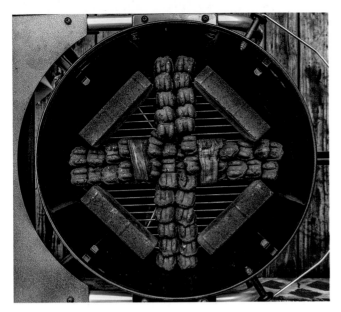

Plus method set up with firebricks.

High Heat, Indirect (The Plus Method)

Another option for indirect high-heat cooking is what I like to call the plus method. This method is easy to use and allows you to cook at a hot, consistent temperature over 300°F/149°C for about three hours. All you have to do is arrange the charcoal, two bricks wide and two layers high, into the shape of a plus sign on the charcoal grate. When forming the plus sign, I like to place a Weber charcoal starter tab in the middle of the bottom layer to make starting the fire easier. Because this is an indirect method of cooking, you'll need a heat shield. Place at least two bricks, ideally four, in the empty regions of the charcoal grate. Place a pizza pan or cooking stone on top of the bricks, so it acts as a heat shield. Light the center of the plus sign so it burns in all four directions at once. Place the cooking grate and lid on the grill. Adjust the vents so that the bottom one is halfway open and the top one is fully open.

Low Heat, Indirect (The Snake Method)

They key to making traditional Southern-style barbecue is to cook at a low temperature for a long period of time. Slow, indirect heat is the preferred cooking method for large or tough cuts of meat that have a high fat content. Over time, this cooking method slowly softens tissue (like collagen and sinew) and melts away layers of fat, basting the meat, which helps create a finished product that is tender and flavorful.

You like ribs that are tender and moist with a sticky, candied glaze? This is the technique that will get you there. It's also great for pork butt, beef brisket and shanks. You can configure your Weber kettle grill for low-and-slow-style cooking using what's known as the snake method. For the snake method, you form a row of charcoal two briquettes wide, along the side of the bottom of the kettle. Then, on top of that row, add another row that is one to two bricks wide. If the outside temps are a little cooler, less than 50°F/10°C, use two bricks for the top row, otherwise you can use one brisk for the top row. DO NOT form the charcoal into a complete ring or circle. Basically, you want to end up with two horseshoe- or C-shaped rows of charcoal. It is important to leave a 6 to 8-inch/15 to 20-cm gap between the two ends of the stacked rows. When you light the double-stacked row of charcoal, the fire will slowly burn from one brick to the next, snaking its way around the base of the grill.

Now, the next part of this technique might seem a little crazy. But stay with me here, and I think you'll be happy to get your hungry on. The secret to making the snake method work is a 21-inch/53-cm pizza pan! Why? Because it acts as heat shield and helps maintain an ambient cooking temperature of about 250°F/121°C. Cooking this way creates a long, slow burn that should easily last for six or seven hours.

To configure your Weber kettle grill so you can cook using the snake method:

IF YOU DO NOT HAVE FIREPLACE BRICKS. one alternative is to use two charcoal baskets to hold up the pizza pan. The charcoal baskets take up more space than the bricks, so just make sure you place them on the grate first and then lay out the charcoal.

FOR AN EVEN LONGER BURN. you can try using the S-shape snake configuration.

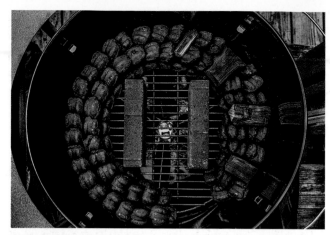

C-method set up with firebricks.

S-method set up with firebricks.

G-method set up with firebricks.

1. Adjust the bottom vent so that it's halfway open.

2. Adjust the top vent so it's fully open.

3. Arrange a horseshoe- or C-shaped row of charcoal, two briquettes wide, that utilizes about 80 percent of the space in the grill.

4. Arrange a row of charcoal, one briquette wide, on top of the previous row of charcoal. If it's cold or windy, you can arrange the snake in two rows, each of which is two bricks, but on warm summer days, the cooking temperature is likely to rise too high.

5. Add about three pieces of smoke wood.

6. Light thirteen briquettes in a charcoal chimney.

7. Dump the hot charcoals on one end of the snake. DO NOT place them on both ends or the snake will burn too fast.

8. Place two fireplace bricks in the kettle. DO NOT use paving bricks intended for walls or walkways. Fireplace bricks are more resistant to heat.

9. Wrap the 20-inch/51-cm pizza pan in aluminum foil.

10. Place the pizza pan on top of the bricks.

11. Place the cooking grate on your kettle.

12. If you're cooking with a temperature probe, place it on the cooking grate close to where you lit the charcoal. This will create a temperature spike very early in the cooking process, but as the snake moves away from the probe, the overall cooking temperature will stabilize. As a result, placing the probe near the beginning of the snake will actually provide a more accurate reading throughout the cooking process. If you place the probe towards the middle of the snake, the temperature will slowly rise as the fire gets closer to the probe.

13. Place a water pan on top of the cooking grate.

14. Place the meat on the cooking grate.

15. After 20 minutes, close the bottom vent so it's open about one-quarter to one-third of the way.

YOU CAN EASILY CONFIGURE your grill for the two-zone cooking method by forming a pile of hot charcoal on one side of the grill. Another way is to use a metal charcoal basket that contours to the side of the grill, which helps keep the hot charcoal confined to one area. Charcoal baskets can also be used to configure your grill for other cooking methods, which we'll talk about later in this book.

TWO-ZONE COOKING

Two-zone cooking uses a combination of direct and indirect cooking methods. Basically, you configure the grill so it has two regions. One half of the grill contains a pile of lit charcoal and acts as a hot zone, while the other half contains no charcoal and acts as a cool zone. With your grill configured this way, you can easily sear meats using direct heat from the hot zone, then move the items to the cool zone, where they finish cooking from indirect heat. Similarly, you can use this setup to slowly cook meats in the cool zone, then, in the final minutes of cooking, finish them off in the hot zone, so their surface becomes slightly charred, crispy and flavorful. Two-zone cooking offers a versatile setup, and one that I think you'll use frequently as your cooking skills improve. This cooking method works well for the following items:

- Chicken thighs and drumsticks
- Chops
- Steaks
- Pork tenderloin

Something to keep in mind about this cooking method is that you have to learn how long different proteins have to remain in each cooking zone. While this might seem daunting at first, I'm pretty sure you'll get the hang of it. Several of the recipes in this book use the two-zone cooking method, so you'll be a pro in no time!

GRILLING TIPS. TRICKS AND BEST PRACTICES

One way you can become a better backyard cook is to cobble together a collection of tips, tricks and best practices. Most of these things are pretty simple, and keeping them in mind when you're first learning to cook on your Weber kettle will quicken the learning curve.

Eliminating Flare-Ups

One problem for a lot of people is flare-ups. Flare-ups are essentially grease fires, caused by fat and oil dripping away from the food you are cooking. If flare-ups repeatedly occur while you are cooking, they'll likely burn food. They might also be a sign

Two-zone set up with charcoal baskets.

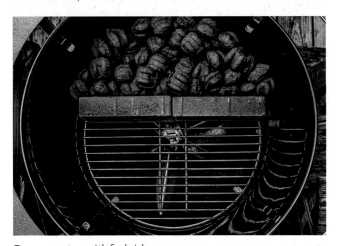

Two-zone set up with firebricks.

that you need to clean the base of your grill. Flare-ups are most common when you cook foods that have a high fat content, such as chicken thighs or sausage.

One way to help minimize the impact of flare-ups begins before you even start to cook. As a general rule, you should try to keep the cooking grate 6 to 8 inches/15 to 20 cm above the hot charcoal. Leaving some distance between the heat source and the food you are cooking lessens the impact of flare-ups when they occur.

Another preventive measure for flare-ups is to simply place the lid on the grill. This helps minimize the amount of oxygen reaching the fire. As you become a better cook, try using the indirect cooking methods discussed in this book, particularly when cooking fattier foods. Finally, as a last resort, you can use a spray bottle to spritz a little water onto the hot charcoal. If you resort to this technique, use caution: Spraying water can spread ash onto the food you're cooking, and using too much water can actually make a grease fire worse.

How to Tell When Meat Is Done

While there are a variety of methods people use to determine when meat has finished cooking, the safest and most accurate way is to use a thermometer. A good practice is to insert the thermometer into the thickest part of the meat. If the food you are cooking has a bone, remember the bone will radiate heat, so you do not want a thermometer touching the bone.

Another technique some cooks use is the finger method. It's somewhat subjective, but offers a tactile way to approximate the texture and sponginess of cooked meat at different temperatures. It goes something like this:

- Touch the fleshy part of your hand below the thumb. That's what raw meat feels like.

- Hold your thumb and middle finger together. That's what meat cooked medium-rare feels like.

- Hold your thumb and ring finger together. That's what meat cooked medium feels like.

- Hold your thumb and pinky finger together. That's what meat cooked well-done feels like.

You should never poke or cut into meat to determine if it has finished cooking. Doing so will lose precious moisture the meat has retained during the cooking process. It can also lead to flare-ups. If you are a new cook just learning to use smoke woods, there is also something you should understand. The smoking process can create a pink color on the surface of meat. While this can give the impression the food is undercooked, properly smoked food is perfectly safe to consume.

USDA Recommended Cooking Temperatures

Don't get porked by pork! For general food safety, you should always cook according to recommendations and guidelines provided by the United States Department of Agriculture (USDA). A thermometer is a useful device that provides an easy way to obtain the internal temperature of food. This helps ensure the food has obtained its minimum internal temperature and is safe to consume. While information is readily available online, I've included the basics in the following table for easy reference.

PROTEIN	MINIMUM INTERNAL TEMPERATURE
Beef, Pork, Veal, Lamb	145°F/63°C
Ground meats	160°F/71°C
Ham	145°F/63°C
Fish and Shellfish	145°F/63°C
Poultry (breasts, whole bird, legs, thigh, wings and ground poultry)	165°F/74°C

Here are some helpful reminders about cooking and temperature that are useful to keep in mind:

- **TEMPERATURE:** Whenever you cook, you should think of the minimum internal temperature as your target temperature. As you become a more experienced cook, you'll learn what temperature you prefer for each type of protein. You'll also learn that when it's one or one or two degrees below the target temperature, it's usually the right time to remove it from the grill.

- **COOKING PATTERNS:** Meat is made up of proteins. As proteins cook, they begin to change in shape, color and texture, often becoming more rigid. By closely observing meat during the cooking process and watching how it reacts as it cooks, you'll learn to evaluate when it's close to done.

- **RESTING:** Depending of the size of the meat you cook, you should let cooked meat rest for a minimum of 5 to 15 minutes. Removing the meat from the heat source and letting it rest allows the protein strands to relax. Resting also helps redistribute the meat's juices so you end up with a finished product that is moist and flavorful. It's important to understand that as a piece of meat rests it continues to radiate heat internally, so its temperature will increase slightly.

Cooking with Sauces and Marinades

I'm willing to bet that culinary schools with fancy French names for things have a sophisticated definition for the word sauce. For me, a sauce is simply a liquid that adds flavor and visual appeal to food. Numerous sauces can be found throughout the culinary world, and many times certain geographic regions are associated with distinct variations. It should come as no surprise that one of my favorite sauces is barbecue sauce. Because barbecue sauce contains a lot of sugar, you should apply it only during the last few minutes of cooking. If you apply a sugary sauce early on in the cooking process, the sugar will burn before the meat finishes cooking.

A marinade is usually an acidic liquid into which you submerge raw meat before it is cooked. The acidic properties help split apart or break up protein fibers, which softens meat and helps it absorb liquid. While marinades can help tenderize a protein, what they're really known for are their flavor enhancing characteristics. Typically, marinades don't penetrate deeply beyond the surface layer, so they work best with thin cuts of meat. Generally speaking, I don't recommend making a marinade more than a day in advance of when you'll use it.

Brining and Injecting

A brine is basically a salty, flavorful water-based solution that acts as a bath for uncooked meat. When you submerge meat into a brine, osmosis occurs, and the salty, flavorful brining solution replaces the water that naturally exists in the uncooked meat. When brining, it is imperative to fully submerge the meat in the brining liquid. For food safety reasons, it's also important to keep the brine at or below 40°F/4°C. While brining enhances flavor, it also adds more salt, so keep this in mind for the finished product. Brining works well for chickens, turkeys and even pork, but I usually don't recommend it for beef.

An injection is a flavorful liquid you add to meat using a syringe. Injections penetrate deeply into large proteins, such as pork shoulder, beef brisket, whole chickens and whole turkeys. Injections can be applied moments before you cook a protein, so I think they're the easiest way to create a finished product that is juicy and flavorful. Something to keep in mind is that many of the herbs and spices injections contain can get stuck in a syringe. It's a good practice to strain injections before you use them.

The Role of Rubs

Rubs are a vibrant mixture of dry herbs and spices you apply to raw meat or seafood prior to cooking. While herbs and spices both come from plants, there is a difference. Herbs are usually flavorful plant leaves, such as thyme, rosemary and basil. Spices are pungent, fragrant seasonings, usually derived from the nonleafy plant regions, like bark, roots or seeds. Examples of spices are fennel, mustard, mace, ginger and pepper. During the cooking process, herbs and spices infuse food with aromas. As meat cooks, fat melts away, and the dry rub forms a savory crust at the meat's surface. While simple to use, rubs provide a great way to enhance the flavor and color of food. One advantage to cooking with rubs is that the overall flavor complexity of the food can be further enhanced with the addition of a sauce.

The Maillard Reaction

The Maillard reaction is creepy chemistry stuff that occurs between sugars and proteins when food reaches over 300°F/149°C during the cooking process. For those of you who enjoy science terms, like lactalbumin and hydroxymethylfurfural, that most people don't understand and can't even pronounce, there is an abundance of information pertaining to the Maillard reaction on the Internet. For the rest of us, the important thing to understand is that the Maillard reaction is what creates the browning effect on the surface of food that results in additional layers of flavor complexity. Examples of this reaction include the char on a steak and the browning of toast. In the end, I think the real secret to cooking is being able to control the temperature of your heat source, understanding how to transfer heat to food and knowing how to enhance the flavor of food. The Maillard reaction is a natural phenomenon that an experienced cook can use to successfully achieve the overall goal of cooking: making great food!

Smoke Woods, Chips and Chunks

In traditional barbecue, a primary component of the basic flavor profile is wood smoke. Essentially, wood smoke is just another flavoring ingredient. If you use too much smoke, the food can taste bitter. If you use too little, the food may be missing just a little something, and fall flat. In addition to learning how much wood smoke to use, you'll also have to learn how to pair different types of wood with various meats and seafood.

Dendrology is the study of trees. While I'm not quite a dendrology kind of guy, I've learned a few things about smoke woods during my time on the competition circuit. Trees are usually classified using two categories: softwood and hardwood. Softwoods are basically trees that have green needles, like spruce or pine. Softwoods generally contain flammable resins. As a result, they should never be used as smoke wood because they'll impart a bitter, acrid flavor into food.

On the other hand, hardwoods offer a wonderful assortment of flavors you can use to enhance the flavor of food. On the competition circuit, hardwoods are usually broken down into two buckets: nut woods and fruit woods. Generally speaking, nut woods pair better with beef, while fruit woods are a better match for pork and poultry. Keep this in mind as you're learning to cook with smoke woods, and try to develop an understanding of the flavor each wood has to offer. As you become more experienced, feel free to mix and match—your personal preference should always be the primary factor in selecting which smoke wood to use. The following table provides descriptions of frequently used smoke woods.

WOOD TYPE	DESCRIPTION
Alder	A mild wood from the Pacific Northwest that is good to use with seafood, poultry, pork and light game.
Hickory	A popular wood that lends a hint of bacon flavor. It goes well with pork and beef.
Mesquite	Typically associated with Texas barbecue, and works well with beef. Use a little at first to get adjusted to its flavor, as mesquite can easily dominate food.
Oak	A milder form of hickory, oak produces a medium smoke flavor that goes well with all barbecue meats, especially beef and pork.
Pecan	An all-around good smoke wood, pecan has a sweet and mild flavor.
Sugar Maple	Frequently found in the Northeast, and a staple on the competition circuit, sugar maple provides a mellow smoke flavor. For an interesting flavor combination, try mixing one or two pieces of this wood with apple or cherry wood. Works well with poultry, pork and cheese.
Walnut	Produces a heavy flavor that lends itself well to beef. I think walnut is best when used alone. If you want to mix flavors, try adding a little fruit wood.
Apple	Perhaps the most common of the fruit woods, apple works well with pork and chicken. Produces a subtle fruit flavor.
Cherry	Creates sweet-tasting smoke that goes wonderfully with pork and poultry. Also offers great color!
Peach	A milder wood that is great for a variety of white and pink meats.

GRILL ACCESSORIES

Weber and other third-party manufacturers sell products designed to enhance your cooking experience. While there are a few things out there that are kind of gimmicky, there are also some excellent products you should consider purchasing if you become a backyard cooking enthusiast.

GRILL GRATE

GrillGrate sells a cooking grate that is manufactured from a thicker gauge metal than the standard cooking grate. This product is more resilient to the wear and tear of backyard cooking. This accessory is used by placing it directly on top of the existing cooking grate and letting it heat up for 10 to 15 minutes. It can be used on any of these recipes that use direct or two-zone cooking techniques

VORTEX

A third-party product designed to deliver a concentrated blast of heat to the cooking grate. When you make wings, this is the perfect way to crisp up skin. How sexy is that?

RAPIDFIRE CHIMNEY STARTER

A round, metal cylinder with a slotted bottom that you use to light charcoal without the need for gross-tasting lighter fluid. Most people start their charcoal chimney by lighting some crumpled-up newspaper or paper towels doused with olive oil beneath the base of the charcoal chimney. Another option is to use a Weber starter cube.

CHARCOAL BASKETS

These D-shaped metal baskets are designed to contour to the curved edge of your Weber kettle grill. Charcoal baskets are usually used to hold hot charcoal in a contained area. This enables you to more easily configure your grill for two-zone cooking or indirect high-heat roasting.

HINGED COOKING GRATE

Made from a heavy gauge metal, similar to the grill grate, this product has two hinged regions that open and close. The hinged cooking grate makes it easier to add charcoal to a charcoal basket and is truly a must-have item for any serious backyard cook.

RIB RACK

A clever device that holds ribs upright, allowing you to cook several racks at one time. Get ready to get your hungry on!

FIREBRICKS

Bricks designed for use in a fireplace that are highly resistant to heat. They're available at fireplace stores and are the preferred way to configure your grill for low-and-slow cooking using the snake method.

PIZZA KETTLE ACCESSORY

Made by KettlePizza, this is a stainless steel insert that turns your Weber kettle into a genuine pizza oven. The design of this will allow for temperatures above 750°F/399°C, which is very close to restaurant pizza ovens.

ESSENTIAL EQUIPMENT

- Grill brush
- Long-handle basting brush
- Metal tongs (without rubber ends so you can move hot charcoal)
- Heat-resistant gloves (welder's gloves are best)
- Thermometer (instant read)
- Injector
- Aluminum foil
- Lighter
- Paper towels
- Hinged cooking grate
- Charcoal chimney

BURGER

You know you have a good hamburger when, after just one or two bites, you have to smack your face with a napkin and then mop up the meat juice running down your hand. A good burger is pretty much the first thing a lot of people think of when they think of cooking in the backyard, so you better be able to deliver. A burger is basically a flattened, panfried meatball served between bread, but to describe it as such strips the burger of its beefy, delicious dignity! For me, the things that make a burger great are a nice char, a pink center and lots of juice.

While many stories discuss the supposed origins of the modern day burger, one I'm particularly fond of can be found in Tulsa, Oklahoma. Residents there talk about Oscar Weber Bilby and claim that on July 4, 1891, he served up the first Angus beef patty on a bun. Hamburgers at a July 4th cookout. Could anything be more American? Nope . . . and now it makes perfect sense why a sandwich with German roots has emerged as an iconic food Americans love!

THE PERFECT BURGER EVERY TIME, PLAIN AND SIMPLE

Ah, the quest for the perfect burger. It's a classic and what many of us strive for. However, a few problems seem to deter you from succeeding in your quest, right? Maybe your burgers get charred on the outside and remain raw in the center because the grill is too hot. Another common conundrum is that they turn into dry hockey pucks. To make the perfect burger, I think there are two important factors to keep in mind: the size of the patty and the proper ratio of lean meat to fat. For a juicy burger that's loaded with flavor, I like to use an 80/20 mix of ground chuck to fat. Just follow this recipe, and you'll complete your quest for the perfect burger each and every time!

YIELD: 4 burgers (8 oz/230 g) **« COOK TIME:** approximately 15 minutes (see in the instructions for preferred doneness)

2 lbs/900 g ground chuck 80/20

Salt and pepper to taste

4 slices of whatever cheese you like (I like sharp cheddar)

4 burger buns

4 tbsp/60 g softened butter

Lettuce and sliced tomato (optional)

> **NOTE:** The USDA says to cook ground beef to an internal temperature of 160°F/71°C. Here is a list of cooking temps for varying degrees of doneness for burgers.
>
> **RARE:** 120°F–125°F /49°C–52°C
>
> **MEDIUM-RARE:** 130°F–135°F/ 54°C–57°C
>
> **MEDIUM:** 140°F–145°F/60°C–63°C
>
> **MEDIUM-WELL:** 150°F–155°F/ 66°C–68°C
>
> **WELL-DONE:** 160°F–165°F/ 71°C–74°C

As part of your quest for the perfect burger, set up your grill for two-zone cooking (page 15). Remember that you need a hot side and cool side. You'll be looking for a dome temperature of 400°F/204°C. Make the proper vent adjustments to obtain your dome temperature. Either lump charcoal or briquettes are fine for this recipe.

Weigh out 8 ounces/230 g of the ground chuck and form it into a ball. Now, don't be too rough with it, because overmixing the meat creates a dense and tough burger, and nobody wants that! After you form the ball, flatten it out to about ¾ inch/2 cm in thickness. Then, take your thumb and put a dimple in the center of the burger. This dimple will help the burger remain flat when you cook it. Repeat 3 more times, and apply salt and pepper to both sides of the burgers.

Sear the burgers on the hot side of the grill. Close the cover to the grill, and cook for 2 minutes. Flip the burgers, and cook for another 2 minutes. Searing quickly cooks the burger, which forms a flavorful char at the surface and helps trap moisture within the meat.

Move the burgers to the cool side of the grill to finish cooking them. After you move the burgers, cover the grill, and don't lift the lid to peak in and check on them. Stay focused, and bring the quest to a glorious conclusion! Let the burgers cook for an additional 5 to 6 minutes for medium-rare, 7 to 8 minutes for medium and 9 to 10 minutes for medium-well. (See side bar for temperature doneness.)

The last few minutes of cooking is the perfect time to melt cheese on your burger. Lay 1 slice of cheese atop each burger, and finish cooking for 2 to 3 minutes. Once the cheese is melted, remove the burgers from the grill. Rest 2 to 3 minutes before eating.

While the burgers are resting is a great time to toast the buns! Spread the softened butter onto the top and bottom of the buns. Place the buns, cut-side down, on the hot side of the grill. Close the cover and wait about 1 to 1½ minutes. Your buns will be lightly toasted.

Assemble your burgers with lettuce and tomato, take a bite and celebrate your victorious quest!

GRILLED BUFFALO TURKEY BURGER

If anyone knows me, then they know that I love anything buffalo style. From buffalo wings, to buffalo cauliflower, to just putting buffalo sauce on my eggs in the morning, it doesn't matter: If you can put buffalo sauce on it, I will! I was trying to figure a way to jazz up the boring old ground turkey burger. You know, I wanted to give it some pizzazz. So I said, "It's pretty close to chicken, so why not throw a little buffalo sauce on it?" After a couple of versions (which were all good), this is what I have as the finished product. If you are a buffalo head like me, then I know you are gonna love it too!

SERVES: 3 « **COOK TIME:** 15 minutes

1 lb/450 g ground turkey (93 percent lean—you need some fat in there)

½ cup/150 g crumbled blue cheese

1 cup/240 ml buffalo sauce (purchase from store or use the recipe on page 48)

3 tbsp/45 g softened butter

3 burger buns

3 leaves green leaf lettuce

3 slices fresh tomato

½ cup/120 ml blue cheese dressing

Set up your grill for two-zone cooking (page 15). Remember that you need a hot side and cool side. You'll be looking for a dome temperature of 400°F/204°C. Make the proper vent adjustments to obtain your dome temperature. Either lump charcoal or briquettes are fine for this recipe.

In a large bowl, add the ground turkey and crumbled blue cheese and mix. Divide the mixture into 3 equal parts and form the burger patties.

Place the burgers on the grate, directly over the hot coals. Close the lid with the vents towards the cool side. Cook for 3 minutes. Remove the lid, flip the burgers, cover and cook for 3 more minutes. Place the burgers onto the cool side, baste with buffalo sauce and cook for 9 minutes or until you obtain an internal temperature of 165°F/74°C.

While you're waiting for the burgers to finish cooking, butter the buns and set them aside until you're ready to toast them.

Remove the burgers and wrap loosely in foil. They're going to rest for only a couple of minutes.

While the burgers are resting, place the buttered buns on the cooking grate directly above the hot coals. Cook for about 30 to 60 seconds, watching closely so they don't burn.

Serve on the buns with lettuce, tomato, blue cheese dressing and more buffalo sauce: hot, buttery, yum!

JALAPEÑO, BACON AND CHEDDAR STUFFED BURGER

Three of my favorite condiments to have with a burger—well, why not stuff them in the burger? Yes that's right, a stuffed burger. The bite from the jalapeño, the sharpness of the cheddar cheese and the smoky flavor from the bacon go absolutely perfectly with a burger. I am going to show you how to make this fan favorite and be the hit at your next cookout!

SERVES: 3 « **COOK TIME:** 20 minutes

1 lb/450 g ground chuck 80/20

1 jalapeño, thinly diced with seeds (remove seeds if you want less heat)

¾ cup/90 g sharp cheddar cheese, shredded

¾ cup/180 g cooked and chopped bacon

3 pretzel burger buns

3 tbsp/45 g softened butter

3 pieces green leaf lettuce

3 slices tomato

Divide the burger in to 6 equal portions. Take each portion and form into a patty. Now, divide the jalapeño, cheese and bacon into 3 equal portions. Place the portioned ingredients onto the center of 3 of the burger patties, top with the 3 remaining patties, pressing the edges to seal. Wrap each burger in plastic wrap and put in the fridge to help with setting up the burger.

Set up your grill for two-zone cooking (page 15). Remember that you need a hot side and cool side. You'll be looking for a dome temperature of 400°F/204°C. Make the proper vent adjustments to obtain your dome temperature. Either lump charcoal or briquettes are fine for this recipe.

Remove the burgers from the fridge and unwrap, sear off the burgers on the hot side of the grill, close the cover to the grill with the vents towards the cool side and cook for 2 minutes. Flip the burgers, cover and cook another 2 minutes.

Take the burgers and put them on the cool side of the grill (cover the grill and don't peek) to finish cooking an additional 10 minutes.

Remove from the grill and let rest for 5 minutes. This is a great time to get those buns ready for toasting. Take the softened butter and spread it onto both the top and bottom buns. Place the buns cut-side down on the hot side of the grill, close the cover and wait about 1 to 1½ minutes. Your buns are now lightly toasted.

Assemble the burger with lettuce and tomato and serve immediately.

MEAT LOAF

I still remember the time my father told me he read about cooking a meat loaf on the grill, without using a pan. "What? Meat loaf plunked right on the grill without using a pan?! You're crazy," I told him. "Won't it fall apart?" Nope, the old man spoke only the truth. I know because I just had to give it a try! Let me tell you, there is something special about smoked meat loaf, and not just because it makes me think of my father. The smoke flavor easily penetrates the ground meat mixture, melding with aromatic spices and herbs, and it all gets coated with a thick, sticky, sweet barbecue glaze. For a nice meat loaf, I like to use a combination of ground beef and ground pork. Typically, I use 1½ to 2 pounds/675 to 900 g of 85 percent lean beef and 1 pound/450 g of ground pork. One bite of a smoked meat loaf, and you'll realize this is a tasty dish lots of people will love!

Side note: To save time, you can use any meat loaf recipe you like and cook it using the method described in this recipe.

SERVES: 4–6 « **COOK TIME:** 50 minutes

2 lbs/900 g 85 percent lean ground beef

1 lb/450 g ground pork

1 cup/120 g Italian-style breadcrumbs

1 large egg

1 tsp/5 ml Worcestershire sauce

¼ cup/60 ml your favorite barbecue sauce, divided

1 tbsp/10 g garlic powder

1 tsp/5 g onion powder

1 tsp/5 g sea salt

1 tsp/5 g black pepper

1 tsp/5 g grated asiago cheese

1 chunk hickory smoke wood

ALTERNATIVE: You can use 2 pounds/900 g of 80 percent lean hamburger mixed with a ½ pound/230 g of pork. I don't recommend using more than ¾ pound/340 g of pork with burger that is 80 percent lean.

In a large bowl, mix all the ingredients together with the ground meat. Use 2 tablespoons/30 ml of barbecue sauce in the mixture. Set aside the other 6 tablespoons/90 ml for use later in this recipe.

Form the meat into 2 halves, roughly oval-shaped, that measure about 4 x 6 inches/10 x 15 cm (forming 2 small loaves shortens the cooking time, compared to 1 large loaf).

Set up your grill for high-heat roasting using charcoal briquettes. If you don't have charcoal baskets, you can use a firebrick to separate the charcoal on either side of the grill. Adjust the bottom vents so the dome temperature reaches approximately 350°F/177°C. Make sure that the hinged side of the cooking grate is over the coals. This makes it easier to add more charcoal during the cooking process, if needed.

Put the smoke wood directly on the hot charcoal.

Place the cooking grate on the grill, cover and heat up for 10 minutes

Using tongs and a paper towel, apply cooking oil to the cooking grate.

Place the 2 meat loaves directly onto the cooking grate in the middle of the grill.

Cook for 35 to 40 minutes. Using a thermometer, check the temperature of the meat loaf. When the meat loaf reaches 145°F to 150°F/63°C to 66°C, brush on the remaining barbecue sauce. Continue to cook until the meat loaves reach 160°F to 165°F/71°C to 74°C, then remove from the grill.

MOO (BEEF)

Sizzle and *hiss*. One of my favorite sounds in the whole world is the sizzle and hiss of raw steak kissing a searing hot grill. In this chapter, we'll discuss several ways to prepare different cuts of beef. One of my favorite ways is actually pretty simple: I like to grill a nice, thick, juicy steak over direct heat to a perfect medium-rare (about 135°F to 140°F/57°C to 60°C). For me, the perfect steak has a cool, pink center, with a nice external crust, and just a hint of smoke flavor. If this sounds good to you, then keep on reading, because we'll have you serving up mouthwatering steaks in no time! If you think grilling steak makes for some tasty goodness, then wait until you see what else is in this chapter. After you learn the basics of direct-heat cooking, we'll discuss reverse searing, and we'll even talk about cooking beef directly on the hot charcoal for a flavor that's out of this world! You ready to fire up your grill and get cooking?

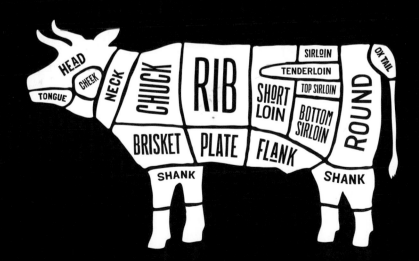

RIB-EYE STEAK

My absolute favorite cut of beef is the rib-eye steak, for a couple of reasons. Rib eye has a decadent, buttery flavor that comes from the fat content in the meat. Rib-eye steaks are cut from the loin muscle, a long muscle that travels along the spine, from the base of the neck to the hip, outside of the rib cage. This region of the animal sees very little movement, so the meat has a delicate texture and is extremely tender. Have I mentioned how much I enjoy rib-eye?

SERVES: 4 « **COOK TIME:** approximately 15 minutes

2 tbsp/30 g kosher salt

2 tbsp/15 g pepper

1 tsp granulated garlic

2 tsp/10 g chili powder

4 boneless rib-eye steaks (at least 1½"/4 cm thick)

¼ cup/60 ml olive oil

1 stick of butter, cut into 8 equal pieces

Set up your grill for two-zone cooking (page 15). Remember that you need a hot side and cool side. You'll be looking for a dome temperature of 375°F to 400°F/191°C to 204°C. Make the proper vent adjustments to obtain your dome temperature. Either lump charcoal or briquettes are fine for this recipe.

Combine all the dry ingredients and put into a shaker bottle. Rub the steaks down with olive oil. Liberally season both sides of each steak with the rub. Let the steaks sit out for about 30 to 45 minutes before you put them on the grill.

Place the steaks on the hot side of the grill for about 3 minutes. If you want the awesome aesthetics of grill marks, rotate the steak about a quarter turn after 1½ minutes. Flip the steak, and continue to cook it on the hot zone for another 3 minutes.

Move the steaks over to the cool side. Add 2 slices of butter to the top of each steak. The butter will melt down, and the steaks will soak in great flavor. Finish cooking until medium-rare (125°F/52°C). This will depend on the thickness of the steaks, but anywhere from 10 to 20 minutes

Remove the steaks and let rest about 5 to 10 minutes.

> **NOTE:** If you have the grill grate accessory, this is a great recipe to use it on. Especially if you want to get awesome looking grill marks. Place the grill grate directly on top of the existing cooking grate above the hot coals and let heat up for 10 to 15 minutes. When heated up, place the steak on the grill grate and follow the above recipe.

SKIRT STEAK COOKED DIRECTLY ON HOT COALS

What the heck is this fool talking about? Cooking a piece of meat directly on top of the hot coals? Yup! I'm serious, and, yes, I can, and it has been done with a good deal of success. The key here is using lump charcoal instead of briquettes. You get a cleaner fire with less ash when using the lump charcoal. A question I usually get is, "Won't the steak burn cooking it this way?" Nope. Because you are cooking right on the coals there is no oxygen to cause flare-ups from the fat drippings. All you need is a little bit of kosher salt, a hot bed of coals and voilà—watch the magic happen.

SERVES: 2 « **COOK TIME:** see recipe instructions for preferred doneness

2 lbs/900 g of skirt steak

1–2 tbsp/15–30 g kosher salt for seasoning

1 tbsp/7 g fresh cracked pepper

Season both sides of the skirt steak with kosher salt and let rest for about 30 minutes before placing on the grill.

Place a cooling rack set in a half-sheet pan.

Fire up one chimney starter with lump charcoal. Once white and ashy, distribute evenly in the lower level of your charcoal grill. Using lump charcoal for this recipe is recommended because it produces less ash and burns cleaner.

Lay steak directly onto the hot coals for 45 seconds. Flip the steak and cook another 45 seconds for rare. Cook for another 60 seconds on each side for medium-rare. Cook for another 75 seconds on each side for medium. And I really hate to say this, but if you want medium-well to well-done, cook it 90 to 120 seconds per side. When finished cooking, immediately place the steak onto heavy duty aluminum foil, wrap and rest for 10 minutes.

Remove the meat from the foil, reserving foil and juices. Slice thinly across the grain of the meat. Return to the foil and toss with the juice.

Serve immediately with some fresh cracked pepper.

REVERSE SEAR NY STRIP STEAK WITH GARLIC BUTTER SAUCE AND GRILLED ONIONS

For many people, a preferred way to cook a steak is the reverse sear method. Basically you're slow cooking the steak first, then hitting it with superhot heat at the end. This cooking method takes a little bit longer than the traditional way, but lots of people think it's worth the extra time! The interior of the steak tends to cook more uniformly—that precious reddish-pink color from top to bottom. At the same time, the final minutes of the cooking process produce a flavorful charred crust on the meat's exterior. Are you hungry yet?

SERVES: 4 « **COOK TIME:** 35–45 minutes

1 stick salted butter

2 sticks unsalted butter

2 cloves garlic, crushed

1 tsp/2 g dried oregano

½ tsp dried basil

¼ tsp coarse ground black pepper

2 strip steaks, 16 oz/460 g (at least 1"/2.5 cm thick)

2 tbsp/30 ml olive oil

1 tbsp/15 g salt

1 tbsp/7 g pepper

Grilled Onions (page 147)

To make the garlic butter sauce, first melt the butter in a small saucepan. Add garlic and sauté until cooked. Add dried oregano, dried basil and black pepper; stir until heated through. Set aside but keep warm.

Set up your grill for two-zone cooking (page 15). Make sure you have a hot zone for searing the steak (at the end of the cooking process) and a cool zone (where you will be starting the cooking process). Adjust the vents on the grill to achieve 250°F to 275°F/121°C to 135°C on the cool side of the cooking grate, where you will be cooking the steak for the first part. Either lump charcoal or briquettes are fine for this recipe.

Rub the steaks down with olive oil. Liberally season both sides of the steaks with salt and pepper. Let the steaks sit out for about 30 minutes before you put them on the grill.

Place the steaks on the cool side of the grill (away from the hot coals). Cover and let cook until the steaks reach an internal temperature of around 125°F to 130°F/52°C to 54°C (medium-rare), usually about 30 minutes. If you like your steak a little more done, keep it on 5 minutes longer for medium, or 10 minutes more for medium-well. Once the steak reaches the desired internal temperature, remove it from the grill, place it on a sheet of aluminum foil and let it rest, uncovered, for about 15 minutes.

During the resting period, leave the cover off the grill. This allows more oxygen to reach the fire so that the coals get nice and hot. After the steak has finished resting, place it on the hot side of the cooking grate, directly over the hot coals. Cook for 1 minute, flip and cook for an additional minute, and the steak is done.

Top with onions and serve with garlic butter sauce on the side for dipping.

TINFOIL STEW

This was one of the first things I ever made cooking over a fire, and it was the catalyst for my love of cooking over fire. I learned this recipe when I was in the Boy Scouts. I remember the scoutmaster walking us through step by step how to assemble it. I couldn't wait to eat it, but needed to wait for it cool down so I wouldn't burn the roof of my mouth off! This was a pretty simple recipe of just beef, potatoes, carrots, onions, salt and pepper cooked in foil packets directly on the hot coals of the camp fire. Well, the recipe has changed slightly, but the cooking method hasn't. This is definitely a dish that the whole family can participate in, and I think you'll have some fun doing it!

SERVES: 4 « **COOK TIME:** approximately 30 minutes

12 sheets approximately 12 x 20 inch/ 30 x 51 cm heavy duty aluminum foil, made into 4 approximately 9 x 9-inch/23 x 23-cm pockets

2 lbs/900 g chuck roast, cut into 1"/2.5-cm cubes

2 tbsp/30 ml olive oil

1 cup/120 g flour

1 lb/450 g small white boiling potatoes (baby yukons), cut in half

4 large carrots, peeled and cut into 1"/2.5-cm chunks

1 medium sweet onion, cut into 1"/2.5-cm pieces

2 cloves garlic, diced

1 cup/240 ml beef stock

¼ cup/60 ml Worcestershire sauce

Salt and pepper to taste

Take 3 sheets of foil on top of each other and fold in half, next you want to seal up each side by making 3 (½-inch/1-cm) folds. You should be left with a nice sized foil pouch open at one end.

For this recipe, I like to use lump charcoal. Also, you will not be using the cooking grate, so set that aside. Set up your grill for direct cooking (page 11). You will want to use about 2 chimneys of lump charcoal. Fill the chimney to the top and light; once the charcoal is ready, dump it into the center of the grill. Fill up the chimney again, and dump the unlit charcoal directly on top of the lit charcoal. Wait about 5 minutes, then place the lid on the grill with all the vents 100 percent open.

While the grill is heating up, place the beef into a large bowl, add the olive oil and mix. Add the flour, toss until evenly coated and discard any unused flour. Next, you want to divide the rest of the ingredients into 4 equal portions.

Add each ingredient to the foil pouch: ¼ of the beef, potato, carrot, onion and garlic. Add 3 tablespoons/45 ml of beef stock and 1 tablespoon/15 ml of the Worcestershire sauce, then salt and pepper to taste.

Seal up the top of each foil pouch. Open the grill and set directly onto the hot charcoal. Cover and cook 15 minutes. Flip each pouch (be careful if using tongs as you don't want to break through the foil), cover and cook another 15 minutes.

Remove from the grill and carefully open the foil pouch. I like to eat directly from the pouch, but you can transfer it to a bowl if you want.

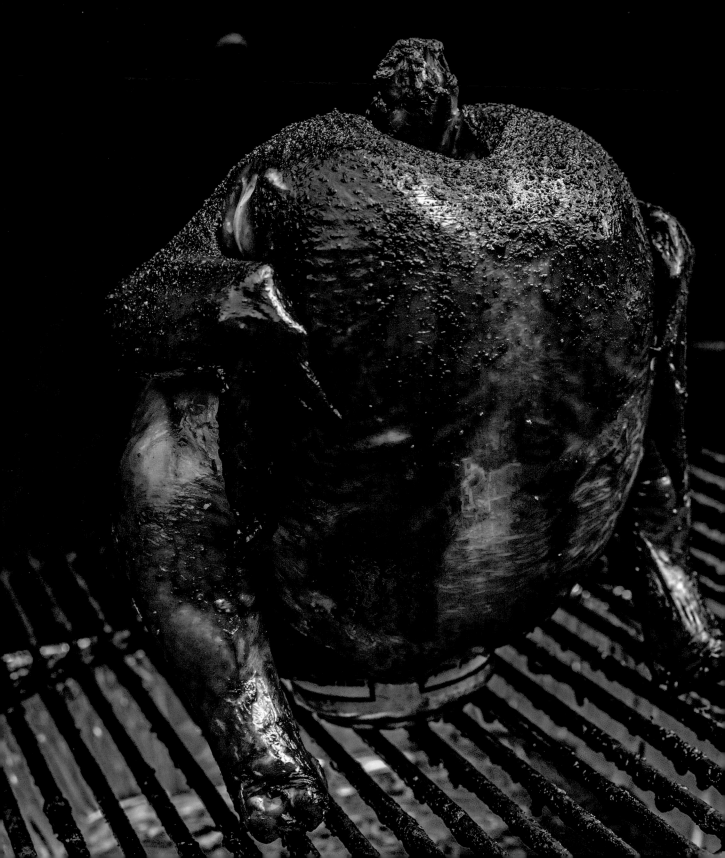

CHICKEN (FOWL)

My favorite things about chicken are the variation and versatility this protein provides. Every part of the chicken is just a little bit different when it comes to flavor and texture, and I like all of them. A whole chicken is actually pretty simple to cook on a Weber kettle. If you configure the grill properly, the process is mostly hands-off, and the entire chicken usually cooks in less than two hours.

You can easily make a meal out of chicken breast or thighs. These regions of the animal cook a little differently, and each has its own flavor. The white breast meat is one of the leanest parts of the animal. It's mild in flavor and easy to dry out but, when cooked right, the breast meat produces what many people think is the best part of the chicken. The thigh meat has a little more fat content, which means you can cook it a little longer, and you don't run as much risk of drying out the meat.

Drumsticks cook quickly and are rather filling. A drumstick is the ideal food to eat with your hands because it has a built-in utensil! Chicken wings are another classic finger food and, almost magically, appear as a great snack or appetizer at parties and tailgating events.

Overall, the flavor profile of chicken is rather subtle compared to pork or beef. This is part of the protein's versatility, and it means there is lots of freedom and creativity for sauces and seasonings. You can use almost anything with chicken: mole sauce, teriyaki, peach glaze and just about anything else that comes to mind. Of all the meats we discuss in this book, I think chicken offers the broadest canvas to experiment with flavor.

CHICKEN DRUMSTICKS

Drumsticks are one of my favorite things to cook on the Weber grill. One reason is that they're versatile—they work with numerous rub or marinade options. Another reason is that drumsticks have a built-in utensil, which makes them fun to eat! I like to cook drumsticks using what I call the seven, three, twenty-one method. You can use this drumstick method anytime you want a quick meal.

SERVES: 4 « **COOK TIME:** 21 minutes

12 drumsticks
¼ cup/60 ml olive oil
3 tbsp/45 g Roadtrip Rub (below)
1 piece of hickory smoke wood

Set up your grill for direct cooking (page 11). Remember to lay out the charcoal evenly to prevent hot spots which can burn the food. Either lump charcoal or briquettes are fine for this recipe. Lightly coat the drumsticks with olive oil. Sprinkle the rub all over the drumsticks.

Place the smoke wood on the grill. Put the cooking grate on the grill, and let the grate heat up for a few minutes. Using tongs and a paper towel, lightly coat the grill with olive oil. Place the drumsticks on the cooking grate, then put the lid on the grill. Cook for 7 minutes.

Remove the lid and rotate each drumstick ⅓ of a turn. Put the lid on the grill, and cook for 7 more minutes. Remove the lid, rotate the drumsticks again. Put the lid on the grill, and cook for an 7 additional minutes.

BOOM! You've just cooked drumsticks using the seven, three, twenty-one method. Who says cooking on charcoal takes a long time? You just cooked dinner in 21 minutes!

ROADTRIP RUB

I remember Tim told me he racked up over six thousand miles on a nine-day drive with his friends. Their only goal was to eat brisket in Lockhart, Texas. But what did a couple of crazy guys who love barbecue do? They also made stops in Kansas City, New Orleans and Memphis! Not too long after Tim got back home, he put together a spice rub that draws inspiration from all the places they visited. One of the things I like about this rub is the dark note the turbinado sugar brings and how it has just a hint of burn at the end. You can use this rub on pork and chicken. It's pretty easy to make. Go ahead and give it a try!

YIELD: 1½ cups (360 g)

4 tbsp/30 g paprika
4 tbsp/60 g turbinado brown sugar
1 tbsp/15 g sea salt
2 tbsp/15 g black pepper
1 tbsp/6 g chipotle or cayenne powder

1 tbsp/6 g cumin
2 tbsp/15 g onion powder
2 tbsp/15 g garlic powder
2 tbsp/4 g dried basil
2 tbsp/4 g dried oregano

Mix all the ingredients together and store in an air-tight container.

BEER CAN CHICKEN

Beer can chicken! It's one of the simplest things to do on the grill and one of my favorite ways to cook chicken. Not only does it look cool, it tastes even better! It's super easy to prepare, which gives you more time to enjoy a nice frosty beverage. While the chicken is turning that beautiful mahogany color on the outside, the inside is being serenaded with that delicious beer, keeping the chicken meat wonderfully moist. The result is a tender and juicy chicken with flavorful and crispy skin!

SERVES: 4 « **COOK TIME:** approximately 1–1½ hours

1 can of your favorite beer (a nice dark lager), 12 oz/355 ml

½ cup/120 g Simple BBQ Dry Rub (page 120), divided

1 whole chicken, 5–6 lb/2.25–2.7 kg

2 tbsp/30 ml olive oil

Set up your grill for high-heat roasting using charcoal briquettes (page 12). If you don't have charcoal baskets, you can use a firebrick to separate the charcoal on either side of the grill. Adjust the bottom vents so the dome temperature reaches about 325°F/163°C. Make sure that the hinged side of the cooking grate is over the coals. This makes it easier to add more charcoal during the cooking process, if needed.

The first thing you want to do is drink about ¼ of the beer. One, beer tastes good, and two, you want to make a little room in the can for some barbecue seasonings. After you've made some room in the can, add about 1 tablespoon/15 g of rub, then give the can a gentle swish to mix the ingredients.

Ready to get weird? Place the can of beer into the cavity of the chicken by lowering the chicken onto the can. The legs should be pointing downward, so that the chicken is upright (kind of like it's supported by a tripod).

Apply olive oil to the outside skin of the bird. Rub it in good, as the oil will provide something for the rub to adhere to. Generously coat the bird with the remaining rub.

Place the can with the chicken in the center of the cooking grate. Cook for 30 to 45 minutes then rotate the bird a ¼ turn to help maintain even cooking. Add 7 charcoal briquettes to each fire. Continue to roast the chicken (another 30 to 45 minutes) until cooked through. Use an instant-read thermometer inserted into the thickest part of thigh, and confirm the meat registers 180°F/82°C. The breast should be about 165°F/74°C. You can tell it's done when you see clear liquid coming out of where you probed it.

Let the chicken rest 10 to 15 minutes before carving.

CHICKEN BREAST

The chicken breast, one the most feared proteins to cook on the grill. Is it cooked all the way through? It's so dry, it tastes like cardboard. Well, no more; from here on out I will show you how to grill chicken breast so it's juicy and tender every time. The key is to brine the chicken and to cook it until the internal temperature is 160°F/71°C.

SERVES: 4 « **COOK TIME**: 15–20 minutes

2 qt/1.9 L cold water

⅓ cup/80 g kosher salt

¼ cup/50 g sugar

4 chicken breasts, trimmed of excess fat

¼ cup/60 ml olive oil

Salt and pepper to taste

1 cup/240 ml Simple BBQ Sauce (page 121) or use your favorite

For the brine, combine the water, salt and sugar; whisk until the salt and sugar are dissolved. Add the chicken and put in the fridge for 45 minutes to 1 hour.

Set up your grill for two-zone cooking (page 15). Remember that you need a hot side and cool side. You'll be looking for a dome temperature of 375°F to 400°F/191°C to 204°C. Make the proper vent adjustments to obtain your dome temperature. Either lump charcoal or briquettes are fine for this recipe.

Remove the chicken from the brine and pat dry with a paper towel. Brush with olive oil and season with salt and pepper to taste.

Place the chicken on the hot side of the grill, cover with dome vents towards the cool side and cook for 3 minutes. Flip the chicken and cook an additional 3 minutes. Move the chicken to the cool side, baste with barbecue sauce and continue cooking for 10 to 15 minutes or until you get an internal temperature of 160°F/71°C.

Remove the chicken from the grill, rest for 5 minutes, then serve.

WINGS

Wings are the ultimate tailgate, party or cookout food that you can grill. They are easy to make, and you can incorporate all sorts of flavors. Here I am going to show you my two favorite methods for cooking wings on the grill.

SERVES: about 4 « **COOK TIME:** approximately 1–1½ hours

¼ stick butter

1 cup/240 ml hot sauce (Frank's RedHot)

¼ cup/60 ml Italian dressing (I like Newman's Own Family Recipe Italian)

Salt and pepper to taste

5 lbs/2.25 kg of wings (flats and drums)

Simple BBQ Rub (page 120)

Simple BBQ Sauce (page 121) (optional)

To make the buffalo sauce, melt the butter in a saucepan. Once the butter is melted, add the hot sauce and Italian dressing. Simmer for 5 minutes. Add salt and pepper to taste. You can make this ahead of time or as the wings are cooking.

METHOD 1: Set up your grill for two-zone cooking (page 15). Remember that you need a hot side and cool side. You'll be looking for a dome temperature of 375°F/191°C. Make the proper vent adjustments to obtain your dome temperature. I like to use briquettes for this because their uniform size helps make an even layer of hot coals to cook on. DO NOT put the cooking grate over the hot charcoal at this time.

Season the wings with the Simple BBQ Rub. Place the cooking grate on your table or counter. Assemble the wings on one half of the cooking grate. Place the grate onto the grill, with the wings directly over the hot coals. Put the cover on, and position the top vent over the cool side of the grill. Cook for 5 to 7 minutes.

Rotate the grate so that the wings are on the cool side of the grill. Using a pair of tongs, flip each wing over, then rotate the grate so the wings are back over the hot coals. Cover the wings (with the vent on the cool side), and cook for 5 to 7 minutes. Rotate the cooking grate so the wings are on the cool side, and finish cooking for 30 to 45 minutes. Check every 15 minutes, and flip the wings around so they cook evenly. You'll be looking for a temperature of at least 165°F/74°C. Remove the wings and toss with either the Simple BBQ Sauce or buffalo sauce. Serve immediately.

METHOD 2: If you happen to have the Vortex grilling accessory, set it up in the middle of the grill on the charcoal grate. Add a full chimney of lit charcoal into the center of the Vortex, using tongs. Briquettes work best for this recipe because of their uniform shape.

Arrange the wings in a circular pattern (flats—skin side up; drums—thicker side away from heat). Place the grate onto the grill, cover the grill with the vents facing you and cook for 15 minutes. Rotate the cover 90 degrees, and cook 15 more minutes. Flip the wings and rotate the cover 90 degrees. Cook for 15 minutes and check for doneness. If not quite crispy enough, cover by rotating another 90 degrees and cook 15 more minutes. At this point, the wings should be fully cooked at 165°F/74°C. Remove from the grill and toss with either the Simple BBQ Sauce or buffalo sauce. Serve immediately.

PORK (SWINE)

Of all the meats I've ever cooked on the grill, I think pork is my absolute favorite! Generally speaking, I find that pork is a naturally salty food—that salt is part of the meat's flavor profile. Many parts of the animal are also fatty. When you slow cook, fat melts down into a savory lather that bastes the meat and adds flavor—kind of like a loving hug the pork momma provides to your taste buds.

Pork comes in a variety of cuts, and I enjoy all of them. Each one is a delicious piece in a magical puzzle of tenderness and delight. Spare ribs, butts and shoulders tend to be tough cuts of meat, so you have to cook them low and slow for a long period of time. The good news is that at low temperatures, pork is very forgiving, so it's a great meat to cook when you're learning the slow-cooking techniques. At the other end of the pork spectrum, you have tenderloin and chops, which are leaner cuts and not as fatty, so you don't have to cook them as long. Then, there is the wonderful bacon. It's fatty and juicy and crispy all at the same time—how could anything be more miraculous?

Pork has a rich taste to it, yet it's also a versatile meat. Various slices of the flavor spectrum complement the finished product. Pork works with earthy flavors, like garlic and onion, or fruity ones, such as pineapple or cherry. It also takes well to sweeteners, like maple syrup or brown sugar, and even acids, like teriyaki or a traditional vinegar-based barbecue sauce served in some southern states.

In the end, a great pork dish comes down to cooking the meat using the proper technique. The good news is that with a little know-how, it's pretty easy to learn to match the right technique to the different cuts of meat. As you work your way through the recipes in this chapter, you'll do just that, and pretty soon all your friends will be calling you a genuine pitmaster!

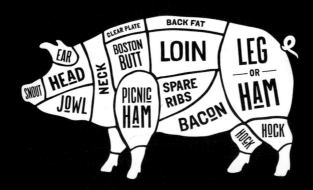

BABY BACK RIBS

When you think all-American barbecue, what do think of ? My first thought is baby back ribs! This is what got me started in the fun and crazy world of competition barbecue. I love ribs! I used to order them every chance I got when we would go out for dinner. Then, one day I thought, *Hmm . . . I bet I could make these at home.* So, I went out and got a smoker. It was a small, red Brinkmann, and the temperature gauge read low, ideal and hot—I'm sure some of you know exactly what I'm talking about. The first set of ribs I cooked came out awful. I think there were only two bones from each rack that were even edible. It was a complete disaster! That was twenty years ago. I have honed my barbecue skills since then, and have come up with a rib recipe that I can certainly be proud of! I think you'll like it, too!

SERVES: about 8 « **COOK TIME:** approximately 3½–4 hours

2 racks of loin back (baby back) ribs with the membrane removed from the back side of the ribs

Simple BBQ Rub (page 120)

3 apple wood chunks

2 cups/475 ml apple juice for spritzing

Simple BBQ Sauce (page 121)

> **NOTES:** If you want to cook more than 2 racks of ribs, you can by using the rib rack as mentioned on page 19. If you decide to use a rib rack, you may have to increase your cook time by 30 to 45 minutes.
>
> Some cooks like to spray ribs with a fruit juice mixture during the cooking process. While it's more common for cooks who use offset smokers, there is no reason you can't give it a try on the grill. Typically, spraying the ribs helps add some nice color, a little bit of flavor and some moisture. Another thing to add to the spritz mixture is cider vinegar and maybe a little dry rub!

Place the raw ribs on a platter or cutting board. Remove the silver skin membrane from the back of the ribs. You can do so using a butter knife and a paper towel.

Now, arrange the ribs with the bones facing up. Apply the dry rub and let sit 10 minutes for the rub to set in. Flip the rack over so the meat side is facing up. Apply the rub and let sit 15 minutes; now apply another coating of rub and let sit another 15 minutes. The ribs are now ready for the grill.

Set up your grill using the C-shape for the horseshoe configuration (page 13). Here is where you want to add the wood chunks. Set the vents so you get a temperature of 250°F/121°C at the cooking grate. A wireless temperature probe is a good investment for applications like this. The iGrill by Weber or Maverick are good choices.

Place the ribs on the grill, meat side up. Let them cook for about 2 hours. After 2 hours, spritz with apple juice. Continue to cook an additional hour, then baste the ribs with some Simple BBQ Sauce. This is going to give your ribs another level of flavor!

Thirty minutes later, you should check to see if the ribs are done. You will know they are done when you can see the meat shrink about ½ inch/1 cm away from the bone. Take the ribs off the grill and loosely wrap in foil. Rest them for about 30 minutes. You want to make sure there is an opening in the foil to let some of the steam out. If you do not vent the steam, you run the risk of the ribs becoming mushy . . . and nobody likes mushy ribs!

Slice the ribs and serve.

APPLE GLAZED PORTERHOUSE PORK CHOP

The porterhouse pork chop, also known as a center-cut chop, is cut from the center of the loin. These chops have both the larger loin on one side of the bone, and the smaller tenderloin on the other side—similar to a porterhouse beef steak. This is one of my favorite cuts of pork, just because there are two different selections of meat contained in the same piece!

SERVES: 4 « **COOK TIME:** approximately 15–20 minutes

½ cup/120 ml apple juice or cider

1 cup/240 g apple butter

¼ cup/60 g Smokin' Hoggz Smoked Apple Wood Dry Rub, divided

4 extra-thick porterhouse pork chops, minimum 1"/2.5 cm thick

1 bottle Lawry's Steak & Chop Marinade

Mix the apple juice or cider with the apple butter and 1 teaspoon of the rub. Store in the fridge until ready to use. You'll use this to glaze the chops during the cooking process.

Place the chops in a zip lock bag and add the marinade, marinate for at least 4 hours to overnight. Remove the chops and season with dry rub.

Set up your grill for two-zone cooking (page 15). Remember that you need a hot side and cool side. You'll be looking for a dome temperature of 400°F/204°C. Make the proper vent adjustments to obtain your dome temperature. Either lump charcoal or briquettes are fine for this recipe.

Place the chops on the cooking grate, directly over the hot coals. Place the lid on the grill, and cook for 2½ minutes.

Remove the lid, flip the chops and baste them with apple glaze.

Put the lid back on the grill and cook an additional 2½ minutes.

Remove the lid, move the chops to the cooler side of the grill, flip and baste with apple glaze.

Let the chops continue to cook with the lid on for 10 to 15 minutes, until the internal temperature reaches 145°F–150°F/63°C–66°C.

Remove and let rest approximately 5 minutes. Serve and enjoy.

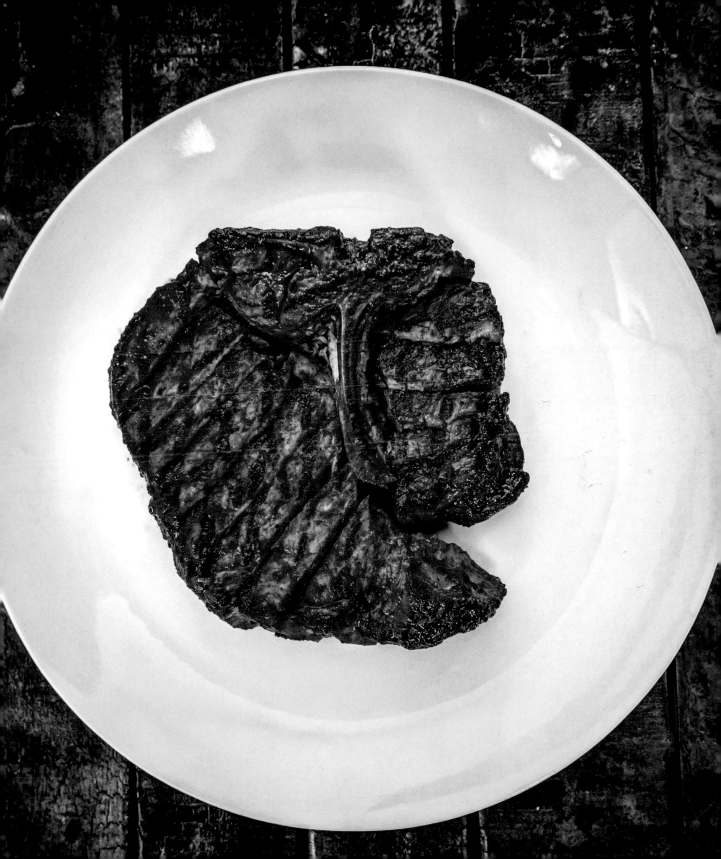

COUNTRY RIBS

Country ribs are a wonderful way to change up what I cook in the yard from time to time. They're from the shoulder region of the animal, right near the loin, so the meat is very tender. Unlike traditional spare ribs, which have large bones, these delightfully meaty pork slabs contain small bones, so they're easy to eat with a knife and fork. That's right—get the cloth napkins ready, baby! One of the goals of this book is to help you become a better backyard cook by learning some basic cooking techniques. This recipe starts off using the indirect high-heat method, then switches to direct grilling to create some flavorful surface char. In about 30 minutes, you'll have this simple but tasty dish complete, so get ready to do some eating!

SERVES: 3–4 « **COOK TIME**: 25–30 minutes

6–8 country ribs

2 tbsp/30 ml olive oil

Salt and pepper

1 chunk apple wood

1 cup/240 ml Simple BBQ Sauce (page 121) or your favorite barbecue sauce

Set up your grill for high-heat roasting using charcoal briquettes (page 12). I like to use 25 charcoal briquettes on each side. If you don't have charcoal baskets you can use a firebrick to separate the charcoal on either side of the grill. Adjust the bottom vents so the dome temperature reaches approximately 350°F/177°C. Make sure that the hinged side of the cooking grate is over the coals. This makes it easier to add more charcoal during the cooking process, if needed.

Coat the country ribs with olive oil. Sprinkle with salt and pepper.

Using tongs and a paper towel, coat the cooking grate with olive oil.

Arrange the ribs, horizontally, in the middle of the grill. Add the smoke wood to the grill. Place the lid on the grill and cook for 8 minutes. Using tongs, flip the ribs and cook for an additional 8 minutes.

Move the ribs directly over the hot charcoal. Let the ribs cook for 2 to 3 minutes, then flip the ribs and cook for 2 to 3 minutes more. This will create a nice char on the surface of the meat. Carefully watch the time when you do this so that you don't overcook these tender pieces of pork.

Move the ribs back to the center of the grill. Brush with barbecue sauce, place the lid on the grill and cook for 3 to 5 minutes.

Using a thermometer, make sure the pork reaches at least 160°F/71°C.

If you want to get even more char on these, place them over the hot coals for about 60 seconds each side.

Remove and serve right away!

PERFECT PORK TENDERLOIN WITH MAPLE CHIPOTLE GLAZE

How many times have you cooked pork tenderloin and it felt like you were eating sawdust? I have your answer right here. So, basically, pork tenderloin is the filet mignon of pork. It's a very lean piece of meat and can dry out very quickly when overcooked, so it needs to be cooked over high heat, and it needs to be done fairly quickly. This is a simple recipe with some great flavors, and it will come out perfect each and every time—no more overcooked, dry pork ever again!

YIELD: 2–3 servings **« COOK TIME:** 18 minutes

½ cup/120 ml real maple syrup

1 tbsp/8 g chipotle powder (if you can't find chipotle powder use regular chili powder)

1 pork tenderloin, approximately 1–1½ lbs/450–675 g

Salt and pepper to taste

Mix the syrup and chipotle powder well and store in the fridge until ready to use.

Set up your grill for two-zone cooking (page 15). Remember that you need a hot side and cool side. You'll be looking for a dome temperature of 375°F to 400°F/191°C to 204°C. Make the proper vent adjustments to obtain your dome temperature. Either lump charcoal or briquettes are fine for this recipe.

Season the pork tenderloin with salt and pepper on all sides. Let sit about 20 minutes. At this point the grill should be ready to cook on.

Place the tenderloin on the cooking grate directly over the coals and put the cover on; cook for 7 minutes. Flip the tenderloin and do the same thing for the other side; do not place it back on the same spot, place it on another hot spot. The reason you don't want to put it back in the same spot is that the spot where the meat was will have cooled down, and you want all the heat you can get on a fresh, new spot. This will allow you to get some nice grill marks. Cook for another 6 minutes. Now take the tenderloin and move it to the other side of the grill (the cool side) where there are no hot coals. With a brush, apply some of the glaze to the tenderloin; cover and cook 2½ minutes. Flip the tenderloin and baste again with the glaze; continue cooking for another 2½ minutes. When the internal temperature reaches about 145°F to 150°F/63°C to 66°C, it's done!

Remove from the heat and let rest about 10 minutes, then slice into ½-inch/ 1-cm pieces and serve.

CUBED PORK BELLY NUGGETS

Wait, did someone say pork belly, on the grill? Yes, indeed! This is probably going to be the best thing you have ever eaten. These beautiful pieces of heaven are melt-in-your-mouth bacon cubes. What makes these things so good? Well, first of all, it's bacon. Secondly, it's bacon, and lastly, it's bacon. This is such a simple recipe to make. Pork belly, dry rub, barbecue sauce and a hint of smoke. Add those ingredients all together, and you have pork belly bliss!

SERVES: 6–8 « **COOK TIME**: 3 hours

4–5 lb skinless pork belly

½–1 cup/120–240 g **Simple BBQ Rub** (page 120)

1 chunk apple wood

1–2 cup/240–480 ml **Simple BBQ Sauce** (page 121) or your favorite barbecue sauce

Remove the pork belly from the package and give it a quick rinse under cold water. Dry it off with a couple of paper towels.

Cut the belly up into 1-inch/2.5-cm cubes. Place into a large bowl and season liberally with the Simple BBQ Rub. Mix well so that each piece is nicely coated

Now, set up your grill using the plus sign set up (page 13). Arrange your firebricks so you can place the foil-covered pizza pan (heat diverter) on top of them. Keep the top vent open and set your bottom vent so that you get a dome temperature of approximately 300°F/149°C.

Leave the cooking grate out of the grill while it's heating up to avoid temperature spikes. The extra airflow when the cover is off will cause the temperatures to rise when placing the food on the grate while still inside the grill.

Place the pork belly pieces in the center of the cooking grate, add your apple wood chunk, then place the grate back onto the grill. Cover and cook for 1 hour.

Place the pork belly pieces in the aluminum pan, put back on the grill, close the lid and cook for 30 minutes.

Cover the pan with heavy duty foil, put back on the grill, close the lid and cook for 1 hour.

Drain grease from the pan, toss the pork belly pieces in sauce, place the pan back on the grill uncovered; close the lid and cook for ½ hour. Open the vents fully to help with crisping up the pork belly chunks.

Remove from the grill and let rest 5 to 10 minutes, serve and enjoy.

PORK LOIN

Pork loin is a long, lean muscle that runs along a pig's back. Because this muscle does not get worked very much during the animal's life, it produces a very tender piece of meat. This makes for great eating, but only if you know the right way to cook it. Cooking pork loin properly is actually simple, and once you learn how, I think you're going to really enjoy this particular cut of pork. On the surface, this pork loin recipe is simple, but simple doesn't mean worthless. Pork loin is fairly lean, so it's easy to dry out or overcook. The key to this recipe is monitoring the meat's temperature as it cooks, and knowing when to remove it from the heat. After the meat is cooked, I want you to focus on two things: the effects of injection and smoke wood. Earlier in this book, I discussed these simple techniques. Now I'm going to draw your attention to how an injection as simple as apple juice helps keeps this lean meat moist and tender, and how cherry wood brings rich mahogany color along with a sweet, balanced smoke flavor to the finished meat. Ready to give this one a try?

SERVES: 8–10 « **COOK TIME:** 1½–2 hours

1 pork loin, 4–5 lb/2–2.25 kg

8 oz/230 ml apple juice

2 tbsp/30 ml olive oil

Salt and pepper

2 cherry wood chunks

Smokin' Hoggz Barbecue Sauce

NOTE: You can cook a beef rib-eye using the same configuration. I usually cook a 4½ to 5 pound/2 to 2.25 kg rib eye roast. Check the rib eye about 45 minutes into the cooking process. Continue to cook until 127°F to 130°F/53°C to 54°C, then remove the rib-eye from the grill. Loosely tent in aluminum foil and let rest for about 20 minutes before serving.

Set up your grill for high-heat roasting using charcoal briquettes (page 12). Set up with 27 briquettes on each side. Once 40 minutes into the cook, add 7 bricks per side. If you don't have charcoal baskets you can use a firebrick to separate the charcoal on either side of the grill. Adjust the bottom vents so the dome temperature reaches approximately 350°F/177°C. Make sure that the hinged side of the cooking grate is over the coals. This makes it easier to add more charcoal during the cooking process, if needed.

Using an injector, inject 8 ounces/240 ml of apple juice into the meat. I like to inject from the top of the pork loin. Inject in a row, every 1½ to 2 inches/4 to 5 cm, for the length of the pork loin.

Lightly coat the pork loin with olive oil. Season with a light coat of salt and pepper.

Place the smoke wood on the grill. Put the cooking grate on the grill, and let it heat up for a few minutes. Here's an easy way to apply oil to the cooking grates to help prevent the food from sticking: Using tongs and a paper towel, lightly coat the grill with olive oil. Place the pork loin in the center of the cooking grate, then put the lid on the grill.

Cook for 1 hour and 15 minutes. Remove the lid and use a thermometer to check the temperature of the meat. If the meat is not at 140°F/60°C, place the lid back on the grill and continue cooking. Check the temperature of the pork loin about every 15 minutes. When the meat reaches 140°F/60°C, brush on some Smokin' Hoggz Barbecue Sauce. Continue to cook for 5 to 10 minutes to let the sauce set. When the pork loin reaches 145°F/63°C, remove it from the grill and let it rest, loosely tented with a sheet of aluminum foil. After 20 minutes, slice, serve and savor! Not such a bad learning experience, right?

GAME MEATS

Have you ever had a relative tell you a story about your spouse that stays with for the rest of your life? My father-in-law, Paul, told me one about my wife, Shaune, and I laugh every time I think of it. One day, when Shaune was about ten, she walked home from school and discovered her father had returned from a hunting trip. She passed an old pickup truck, and as she made her way up the driveway, she spotted something she'd never forget. Hanging upside down from a rope, right in the center of the garage, was a deer that had been cut down its center and had blood draining from it. Shaune's brothers thought it was exciting, but it turned her stomach so badly that she didn't stick around for any more of the butchering. That evening, she ventured back outside to join her family for some grilled meat, without understanding what it was she was eating. To this day, one of my wife's favorite dishes is a venison chop wrapped in bacon—but she still doesn't like to be around when it's being prepared.

Game meats, like venison, are quite lean, so you have to be precise and attentive when cooking them. These meats contain very little fat to render out, so they're easy to overcook. Typically, I recommend cooking game meats no higher than medium. Because the meat is so lean, it easily toughens, even when you let it rest. I think it's best to plate and serve game meat immediately after it finishes cooking.

This chapter includes recipes for duck, lamb, turkey and venison. While a lot of people might not cook these items too often, I'm including them to help encourage you to push beyond your comfort zone and become a better backyard cook. With just a little practice, you'll learn there is nothing to be afraid of when preparing these lean and flavorful meats. In fact, it won't be long before you discover how advantageous it can be to befriend a hunter who understands that you know how to cook game meats!

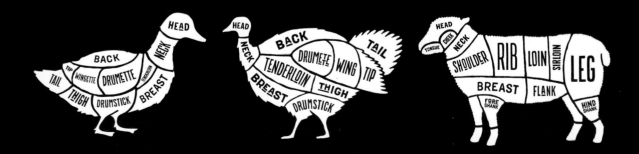

GRILLED DUCK BREAST

When looking for duck breast, you want to look for plump evenly shaped breast with thick, creamy-white skin. A well-grilled duck that's crispy on the outside and moist and flavorful in the middle is, after all, hard to beat.

SERVES: 2 « **COOK TIME:** approximately 20 minutes

2 duck breasts

1 tbsp/8 g Chinese five-spice powder

2 tbsp/30 ml honey

3 tbsp/45 ml light soy sauce

1 tbsp/15 ml fresh lemon juice

To prep the duck breast, score the fat on the duck breast in crisscross/diamond patterns at 1-inch/0.5-cm intervals.

Mix the five-spice powder, honey, soy sauce and lemon juice. Place the duck breasts in a bowl and pour the mixture over the duck. Cover and marinate at least 1 hour at room temperature or up to 24 hours in the refrigerator, whichever is more convenient.

Set up your grill for two-zone cooking (page 15). Remember that you need a hot side and cool side. You'll be looking for a dome temperature of 375°F to 400°F/191°C to 204°C. Make the proper vent adjustments to obtain your dome temperature. Either lump charcoal or briquettes are fine for this recipe.

Remove the duck breasts from the marinade, reserving the marinade for sauce, if desired. Place the duck breasts on the cooking grate directly over the hot coals, skin-side down, and sear for about 2 to 3 minutes, just until the skin is well browned.

Place the duck onto the cooler side of the grill, skin-side up, and continue to cook for 12 to 17 minutes. If you want it medium-rare, cook until 135°F/57°C, medium 145°F/63°C and medium-well 155°F/68°C.

While the duck is cooking, take the remaining marinade and heat it up in a saucepan for about 5 minutes. Set it aside until ready to use.

Remove the duck from the grill once you've reached your desired doneness and let rest for 5 minutes. Slice the duck breasts on an angle half an inch/1 cm thick. Pour the heated sauce over the top and serve.

LAMB CHOPS

You either love them or hate them; there is no in between. I love them, and, thankfully, my wife does too! Something else I love is that lamb chops are so easy to make. I also love my wife . . . even more than lamb chops.

SERVES: 4 « **COOK TIME:** 5–6 minutes

2 large garlic cloves, crushed

1 tbsp/2 g fresh rosemary leaves, finely chopped

1 tsp/1 g fresh thyme leaves, finely chopped

1 tsp/5 g kosher salt

2 tbsp/30 ml extra-virgin olive oil

8 lamb chops about ¾"/2 cm thick

Place all the ingredients in a bowl (except the lamb) and mix well

Rub the mixture/paste all over the lamb chops, wrap in plastic wrap and put in the fridge for 1 hour.

While the lamb is soaking up all that great flavor from the marinade, go and set up your grill for direct heat grilling (page 11), remembering to spread out the hot coals evenly. You want a dome temperature of about 400°F/204°C. Either lump charcoal or briquettes are fine for this recipe.

Place the chops onto the cooking grates, directly over the hot coals, and cook for 2½ minutes. Flip and cook an additional 3 minutes for medium-rare (125°F to 130°F/52°C to 54°C) or 3½ minutes for medium (135°F to 140°F/57°C to 60°C).

When the desired temperature is reached, remove the chops from the grill and rest for 5 minutes.

MUSTARD AND HERB CRUSTED GRILLED RACK OF LAMB

A rack of lamb is the perfect size for two people. Or, if you are hosting a party, it can be a great appetizer, because you can cut them into individual chops. I usually cook lamb for special occasions like holidays and anniversaries. The great thing about buying lamb today is that the bones are already cleaned of excess fat and gristle, which makes prep a piece of cake! Below is a very simple recipe that's easy to make and delicious to eat!

SERVES: 2 « **COOK TIME:** approximately 20–25 minutes

2 cherry wood chunks

1 bone-in rack of lamb, trimmed and frenched (all the fat is trimmed from the bone, making it like a handle)

Salt and pepper to taste

2 tbsp/30 ml Dijon mustard

2 tbsp/30 ml olive oil

1 tbsp/2 g chopped flat-leaf parsley

2 tbsp/15 g chopped rosemary

2 tsp/2 g chopped thyme

Set up your grill for two-zone cooking (page 15) using your cherry wood chunks. Remember that you need a hot side and cool side. You'll be looking for a dome temperature of 375°F to 400°F/191°C to 204°C. Make the proper vent adjustments to obtain your dome temperature. Either lump charcoal or briquettes are fine for this recipe.

Season the lamb with salt and pepper and combine the mustard, oil, parsley, rosemary and thyme to make a paste. Rub the paste all over the meat portion of the lamb. Place in the fridge and let sit for about 1 hour.

Remove from the fridge and let sit out for ½ hour.

If you want, you can wrap the top of the bones with foil. This will help prevent the bones from burning. If you're not trying to impress anyone and don't mind the bones getting a little dark in color, just leave them be.

Place the lamb on the cooking grate directly over the hot coals, meat-side down. Cover and cook for 3 minutes, until the meat is nice and seared; flip and cover and cook an additional 3 minutes.

Move the lamb over to the cool side of the grill and continue to cook until they are at 145°F/63°C—about 15 minutes.

Remove from the grill and let the rack rest 5 minutes.

To serve, slice in between the bones, making them into chops.

 # TURKEY

Cooking a whole turkey on the grill? Yes, absolutely! In fact, smoked turkey happens to be my mother's favorite backyard meal. So much so, that every Mother's Day, we cook a smoked turkey for Mom—because she's the best mom in the whole world!

SERVES: approximately 8 « **COOK TIME**: approximately 2½–3 hours

1 fresh turkey, 12–14 lb/5.4–6.3 kg

1 stick butter, cut into 8 pieces

Olive oil

Fresh ground pepper

Kosher salt

2 medium carrots, cut into ½"/1-cm pieces

2 celery stalks, cut into ½"/1-cm pieces

1 small onion, cut into ½"/1-cm pieces

1 cup/240 ml chicken stock

2 chunks apple wood

Prepare the turkey by taking it out of the packaging and removing the bag of giblets. Save the giblets for later so you can make giblet gravy. Remove any excess skin around the openings and rinse off the bird.

Take 8 slices of butter and put them under the skin on top of the breast meat, 4 on each side. Rub the turkey all over with a very thin layer of olive oil. Sprinkle with fresh cracked pepper and kosher salt.

Set up your grill for roasting, using charcoal briquettes (page 12). If you don't have charcoal baskets, you can use a firebrick to separate the charcoal on either side of the grill. Adjust the bottom vents so the dome temperature reaches approximately 350°F/177°C. Make sure that the hinged side of the cooking grate is over the coals. This makes it easier to add more charcoal during the cooking process.

In the roasting pan, add the veggies and chicken stock. Place the pan in between the charcoal and the cooking grate. Place the turkey on the cooking grate above the pan, breast-side up. Add your wood chunks on top of the hot coals. Cook for 1 hour. At this point you should have some nice color on the skin of the turkey. To preserve that color, cover the turkey with heavy duty foil and cook an additional 1 to 1½ hours or until the internal temperature of the breast (white meat) is 165°F/74°C and the thigh (dark meat) is 180°F/82°C.

Remove and let rest about 20 minutes, loosely tented with aluminum foil. Carve it up and serve.

GRILLED LOIN OF VENISON

I remember the first time I had venison. I was at my aunt and uncle's summer cottage for a family cookout. There was this big ole pot of American chop suey made with ground venison. I just thought it was ground beef. It wasn't until I had finished my plate that I was told it was venison. I should have known, because I also remember going to my uncle's house in the fall, and there would be a deer or two hanging from the garage rafters. There was no shortage of venison at their house. Unlike the beef that we are used to, venison is very lean (not a lot of fat), meaning that when you cook it, it can overcook very quickly and become dry, gray and livery, and that's not very fun. Here I will show you how to cook venison perfectly every time—a nice char on the outside and pink on the inside!

SERVES: 2–4 « **COOK TIME:** approximately 15–20 minutes

1 venison loin/roast, 1–1½ lb/450–675 g

¼ cup/60 ml olive oil

1 tbsp/15 g salt

¼ cup/60 ml Simple BBQ Sauce (page 121) or your favorite barbecue sauce

Coat the venison loin with olive oil and salt well. Set aside for 20 minutes at room temperature.

Set up your grill for two-zone cooking (page 15). Remember that you need a hot side and cool side. You'll be looking for a dome temperature of 375°F to 400°F/191°C to 204°C. Make the proper vent adjustments to obtain your dome temperature. Either lump charcoal or briquettes are fine for this recipe.

Place the venison on the cooking grate directly over the hot coals; keep the grill cover open. Let this cook 5 to 8 minutes without moving, depending on how hot your grill is and how thick your venison loin is. You want a good sear, with good grill marks, on that side of the meat. Flip and repeat on the other side, cooking an additional 5 to 8 minutes, brushing that side with barbecue sauce.

The reason for keeping the grill cover off during the cooking process is there is not a lot of fat in the meat so it will not cause any flare-ups and burn the meat, plus you'll be able to get that beautiful char on the outside.

You'll be looking for an internal temperature of 145°F/63°C. If the venison needs some more time, turn it to sides that have not had direct exposure to the grill and cook for 2 to 3 more minutes, checking all the way. Brush those sides with barbecue sauce, too.

When the meat has been cooked to your liking, take it off the fire and let it rest, tented with foil, for 10 minutes.

Serve with barbecue sauce on the side.

> **NOTE:** This recipe will work with any other lean game meat, such as elk, antelope, moose, bison or even a beef filet mignon.

SAUSAGE
AND TUBE STEAKS

The crack of the bat, the cheer of the crowd and the hot dog in hand. A German immigrant named Christian von der Ahe, who owned the St. Louis Browns in the late 1800s, is central to an early connection between baseball and hot dogs. In fact, some people claim he was the first person to sell hot dogs at a baseball game. Hot dogs are also known as a frankfurters, a word that appears to be connected to Frankfurt, Germany—a city where ground meats mixed with flavorful spices and formed into links has a lengthy history dating back centuries. In the United States, hot dogs, sausages and bratwurst, known as tube steaks, are typically thought to have been introduced by German immigrants. This chapter includes recipes that focus on a variety of tube steaks, so that the next time you step up to the grill at a family outing, you can be sure you'll hit a home run!

Hot dogs can be served with a variety of toppings, and certain cities are known for serving up dogs a particular way. One thing that really rounds out the hot dog experience is the bun. I think hot dog buns are best lightly toasted and caressed with a hint of butter. In New England, hot dogs are usually served on split-top rolls, sliced ¾ of the way into the bun. Top-loaders are easy to hold, wrap the dog on three sides and allow you to stack layers of condiments right on top of the dog. Most other parts of the country serve dogs on hinged buns, sliced lengthwise, which makes for messier eating. No matter how you slice it, the hot dog has emerged as an American classic!

GRILLED HOT DOGS

Alright, I know what you're thinking: Seriously, he's doing a recipe for grilled hot dogs? Yes, I am. Why? Because too many times I've been to cookouts where the hot dogs look like they were cooked in a volcano, or wondering if they've been cooked at all! LOL! I believe that the quality of the hot dog matters. I like to use 100 percent all-beef hot dogs. Why? Because I like the flavor better. So sit back, relax and watch the magic happen.

SERVES: 8 « **COOK TIME:** approximately 10 minutes

1 package all-beef hot dogs

1 stick softened butter

1 package hot dog buns

Ketchup

Yellow mustard or brown spicy mustard

Dill or sweet relish (I prefer dill)

1 sweet onion, diced

Set up your grill for two-zone cooking (page 15). Either lump charcoal or briquettes are fine for this recipe. Remember that you need a hot side and cool side. You'll be looking for a dome temperature of 400°F/204°C. Make the proper vent adjustments to reach your desired dome temperature.

Place your hot dogs on the cooking grate directly over the hot coals. It is very important at this step to watch them closely. Hot dogs burn very fast and can turn black in no time. To prevent that, you have to keep them moving every 30 seconds. To help keep them moving, place them perpendicular to the lines on the cooking grate, so you can roll them more easily and get those nice grill marks!

Once you get those nice grill marks, about 3 to 4 minutes, move the hot dogs over to the cool side of the grill to finish. Cover the grill and cook about 5 to 6 minutes.

Hot dogs are fully cooked straight out of the package; the idea at this step is to make sure they are heated through and to get a little more color on them.

This is a great time to get those buns ready for toasting. Take the softened butter and spread it onto both sides of the buns. Set aside until the hot dogs come off the grill. Place the buns on the hot side of the grill, close the cover and wait about 30 seconds to 1 minute. Flip the buns and cook another 30 seconds to 1 minute. Your buns are now lightly toasted.

Remove the buns from the grill, place a hot dog in each roll, apply toppings like ketchup, mustard, dill, relish or sweet onion, and serve.

PERFECTLY GRILLED BRATS AND SAUSAGE

What's a summertime cookout without grilled sausage? Boring, right? Every cookout I've ever been to has had some sort of grilled sausage. Now, I love sausage just as much as the next guy, but I'm always disappointed because at most cookouts, sausage tends to be overcooked and dry. Well, not anymore! The key to perfectly grilled sausage is paying attention to that internal temperature (cook to 165°F/74°C). Now, some people say, "You have to parboil sausages before you grill them." And to that, I say, "Ugh!" Well, that's total BS in my book. Basically, what you'd be doing is making sausage water. A lot of the flavor would be boiled out, gone, and all you'd be left with would be boring, bland, flavorless sausage. By sharing some insights, I am going to show you how to get juicy and delicious sausage each and every time. It's easier than you think. Are you ready?

SERVES: 8 « **COOK TIME:** approximately 15–20 minutes

8 Italian sausages or brats

8 hot dog/sausage buns

Grilled onions and peppers

1 bottle brown and spicy mustard, 12 oz/355 ml

NOTE: When cooking sausage, I like to aim for a target temperature of 160°F/71°C. I think cooking the sausage to a higher temperature renders too much fat from the ground pork, which results in a dry finished product, lacking in flavor. A cooked sausage should not be pink at its center.

Set up your grill for two-zone cooking (page 15). Either lump charcoal or briquettes will work fine for this recipe. When cooking sausage, remember that you need a hot side and a cool side of the grill. You want a dome temperature of 400°F/204°C. Make the proper vent adjustments to reach the temperature.

When the grill is at the target temperature, place the sausage on the cool side of the cooking grate. Place the lid on the grill, with the vent over the sausages. Cook for 7 to 8 minutes. Remove the lid and flip the sausages. Place the cover on the grill, vent over the sausages and cook for an additional 7 to 8 minutes.

At this point, the sausages should be browning up nicely and getting close to the desired internal temperature of 165°F/74°C. So here is where we will finish them with a nice sear on the hot side of the grill. Do not use a fork for this step. I know it's easy just to stab with a fork, but if you do that, then all the juiciness will come squirting out and leave you with a dry sausage. Furthermore, all those juices will cause your grill to flare up and burn the food. And nobody wants flare-ups or burnt food.

Using tongs, move the sausages to the hot side of the grill. Cover and cook for 1 to 2 minutes, keeping a close eye on them, making sure they don't burn. Flip them over and cook another 1 to 2 minutes.

Remove the sausages from the grill, and let them rest for 5 to 10 minutes before serving.

Serve on buns with the grilled onions, peppers and mustard.

STUFFED SAUSAGE FATTY

The sausage fatty has become one of the more popular things to cook at a barbecue contest. A fatty is sort of like a calzone, but, instead of dough, the outer layer is ground pork. Fatties are simple to make, flavorful and just plain delicious! Once you learn how to make a fatty, you'll quickly see that the combination of ingredients you can use is nearly endless. They're also a good way to bring about a smile when you're using up leftovers. This particular recipe is a rich and savory fatty that is one of my favorites!

SERVES: 4–8 « **COOK TIME:** 2 hours

1 package ground breakfast sausage (Jimmy Dean)

1 lb/450 g ground, sweet Italian sausage

Smokin' Hoggz Smokey Apple Wood Dry Rub

1 package cream cheese, 8 oz/230 g

½ cup/150 g pickled jalapeños, diced

Simple BBQ Sauce (see page 121)

1 chunk of fruit wood, optional

Mix together the breakfast sausage and the Italian sausage. Put the mixture into a 1-gallon/3.8-L bag. Flatten it out, spreading the mixture uniformly, until it reaches all sides of the bag. The mixture will be approximately ½ inch/1 cm thick.

Spray a sheet of aluminum foil with non-stick cooking spray. Take the mixture out of the bag and place on the sheet of foil.

Season the surface of the sausage mixture with dry rub. Break the cream cheese into ½-inch/1-cm pieces and place onto the sausage. Add the jalapeños.

Roll the entire thing into a log, and completely season the outside with dry rub.

Place the fatty onto another sheet of aluminum foil, and roll into a nice tight log. Twist the ends of the foil making it look like a large Tootsie Roll. Put in the fridge for about 1 hour to set and form.

Set up your grill for two-zone cooking (page 15). Remember that you need a hot side and cool side. You'll be looking for a dome temperature of 350°F to 375°F/177°C to 191°C. Make the proper vent adjustments to reach your desired dome temperature. Lump charcoal or briquettes are fine for this recipe.

Remove the fatty from the fridge and place onto the cooking grate on the cool side of the grill. If you want to add a little smoky flavor, add one chunk of fruit wood such as apple or peach at this time.

Place the cover on the grill, with the vents over the cool side. Cook for about 30 minutes. Remove the lid, turn the fatty 180 degrees, cover and cook an additional 30 minutes. Brush with Simple BBQ Sauce and cook until the internal temperature reaches 150°F/66°C, approximately 30 to 60 minutes.

Take the fatty off the grill and let it rest for about 15 minutes. Slice into 1-inch/2.5-cm slices, serve and smile as your guests devour this delicious sausage masterpiece.

FINZ AND SHELLZ

Growing up in New England, my family ate a lot of cod and haddock. It was always cooked inside, baked in the oven. It wasn't until I started competing in grilling contests that my family cooked fish outdoors. Grilled seafood has a different flavor. It goes back to that whole char thing for me, and that slightly smoky flavor that grilling adds to food. I look forward to seeing the expressions on people's faces when they have grilled seafood for the first time. They're like, "Wow, where has this been my whole life!"

Seafood is special to me, and not just because of my New England roots. The first time I heard my name called for first place at a grilling contest, it was for salmon. This chapter includes recipes for some of my New England favorites, like shrimp, scallops, lobster and cod. Seafood is another type of food that usually cooks in the grill in a matter of minutes. Once you learn the basics, you'll be able to cook up a seafood feast capable of making Squanto smile.

GRILLED COD LOIN BLACKENED

Cod can be a large fish, and the fillet is often too big for a single portion. However, it is possible to buy just the cod loin, which is cut from the middle section or fattest part of the fillet. Succulent loins are short and fat compared to longer cod fillets, and they are considered the prime cut. This is a pretty simple recipe with a nice light flavor.

SERVES: 4 « **COOK TIME:** 8–10 minutes

2 tbsp/15 g paprika

2 tbsp/15 g onion powder

2 tbsp/15 g garlic powder

1 tbsp/8 g chili powder

3 tsp/15 g kosher salt

2 tsp/4 g black pepper

2 tsp/4 g white pepper

2 tsp/7 g ground cumin

1 tsp/3 g ground cayenne pepper

1 tsp/3 g ground mustard

⅛ tsp ground nutmeg

2 cod loins

Olive oil

Mix all the seasonings well and store in an air tight container until ready to use.

Set up your grill for direct cooking (page 11). Remember, when spreading the charcoal out in the bottom of the grill, to have a nice, even layer of hot coals. Set your top and bottom vents so you get a dome temperature of approximately 400°F/204°C. Lump charcoal or briquettes are fine for this recipe.

Place the cod loin on a flat surface. Pat dry with a paper towel. Lightly brush both sides of the loin with olive oil. Season both sides with the blackening seasoning and keep in the fridge until ready to use. If you like it spicy, use more seasoning; if you don't like it as spicy, use less.

Once the grill is ready, place the cod loins on the cooking grate directly over the hot coals; cook for 4 to 5 minutes, flip and cook an additional 4 to 5 minutes. To test for doneness, poke with a fork into the thickest part of the fish, then gently twist the fork and pull up some of the fish. Undercooked fish resists flaking and is translucent. If your fish is undercooked, just continue cooking it until it is done.

Remove from the grill and let rest for 5 minutes.

Serve and enjoy.

> **NOTE:** Other white fish with a similar texture and taste such as pollock or haddock can be used in many recipes that call for cod.

GRILLED LOBSTER TAIL

One of things us New Englanders are known for is seafood, especially lobsters; it's pretty much a staple at any cookout during the summertime. Keeping the flavors simple, like salt, pepper and melted butter will allow you to enjoy the sweet taste of the lobster. I also like grilling lobster tails removed from the shell, because you get a little bit of char on the meat that goes great with the melted butter.

SERVES: 4 « **COOK TIME:** approximately 6–8 minutes

4 lobster tails, 6–8 oz/168–230 g

4 long wooden skewers

Salt and pepper to taste

1 cup/240 ml melted butter

Set up your grill for direct cooking, this time using lump charcoal (page 11). Remember, when spreading the charcoal out in the bottom of the grill, you should have a nice even layer of hot coals. Set your top and bottom vents so you get a dome temperature of approximately 400°F/204°C.

The first thing you want to do is remove the meat from the shell. Turn the tail on its back, the underside facing up, and with a pair of kitchen shears, cut down both sides of the shell, all the way to the end. Gently remove the meat from the shell with your fingers.

Lay out each tail, and from one end insert the wooden skewer all the way through to the other side. Using the skewer will prevent the tail from curling up into a ball when cooking.

Season each tail with salt and pepper.

Place the tails on the cooking grate, cover and cook over direct heat for about 3 to 4 minutes, flip the tails and cook another 3 to 4 minutes or until you reach an internal temperature of 135°F/57°C.

Remove from the grill and serve immediately with the melted butter.

> **NOTE:** Removing the skewer from the tail is fairly easy, hold the tail down with a fork or your hand; with your other hand, grab the end of the skewer, twist until the skewer releases and pull straight out.

GRILLED SHRIMP COCKTAIL

We are very familiar with the traditional shrimp cocktail, which is served cold. Well, this one is grilled, and it's served hot with an incredible cocktail sauce that has just a hint of heat. This recipe will teach you how to grill shrimp to perfection each and every time.

SERVES: 3–4 « **COOK TIME:** 4 minutes

1 cup/240 ml ketchup

¼ cup/60 g prepared horseradish

2 tsp/10 ml Worcestershire sauce

1 tbsp/15 ml hot sauce (I like Franks, if you don't like it too spicy leave it out or adjust to taste)

½ tsp salt

¼ tsp pepper

1 lb/450 g uncooked shrimp, peeled and deveined

5–6 wooden or metal skewers

Smokin' Hoggz Smokey Apple Wood Rub (or your favorite seafood seasoning)

To make the cocktail sauce, mix the ketchup, horseradish, Worcestershire sauce, hot sauce, salt and pepper, and store in an airtight container in the fridge until ready to use.

Set up your grill for direct cooking, using lump charcoal (page 11). When spreading the charcoal out in the bottom of the grill, remember to create a nice even layer of hot coals to help prevent hot spots. Adjust your top and bottom vents so you get a dome temperature of approximately 400°F/204°C.

Take the shrimp one by one and slide them onto the skewers. Typically, you should be able to get 4 to 5 shrimp per skewer. Season both sides of the shrimp with the rub or seasoning.

Place the shrimp skewers on the grill grates, cover and cook for 2 minutes. Remove the lid, flip the skewers, cover and cook for an additional 2 minutes. Shrimp cook very fast and in the blink of an eye can be overcooked. You'll want to cook them just until the shells turn pink and the shrimp are opaque.

Remove the shrimp from the grill and serve with cocktail sauce.

PERFECT SALMON
METHOD I: INDIRECT

Salmon is one of my favorite types of fish to cook on the grill, and it's easier to prepare than you might think. I am going to show you two different methods for cooking salmon on the grill that I'm sure you are going love and will be cooking all the time. The first way is indirect (two zone) and the second is cooking it on a cedar plank with lemon and dill directly over the coals. I know you're itching to get rolling! So, let's go!

SERVES: 4 « **COOK TIME:** approximately 20–25 minutes

2 lb/900 g salmon

¼ cup/60 ml maple syrup

Smokin' Hoggz Apple Wood Smoke Rub

¼ cup/55 g brown sugar

1 chunk sugar maple wood (apple and peach woods are good too)

Set up your grill for two-zone cooking (page 15). Remember that you need a hot side and cool side. You'll be looking for a dome temperature of 375°F to 400°F/191°C to 204°C. Make the proper vent adjustments to obtain the dome temperature. Lump charcoal or briquettes are fine for this recipe.

Cut the salmon into 4 servings of 8 ounces/240 ml, leaving the skin on. Apply approximately 2 tablespoons/30 ml of maple syrup over each piece, sprinkle on the dry rub and then apply 2 tablespoons/30 ml of brown sugar. Let the salmon sit in a container in the fridge for about an hour.

For salmon, I like to use mild fruit woods because I want to taste the natural flavor of the fish with just a hint of smoke.

Place the salmon on the cool side of the grill, and add your smoke wood. Place the cover on the grill with the lid vent towards the cool side. Cook for 20 minutes or until you get an internal temperature of 125°F to 130°F/52°C to 54°C (medium). If you like your salmon a little more cooked, keep it on for another 5 minutes or until you get an internal temperature of 135° to 140°F/57°C to 60°C.

Remove from the grill and serve right away.

> **NOTE:** The FDA recommends the internal temperature of cooked salmon to be 145°F/63°C, but to get a flakier, moist and tender piece of salmon, most cooks/chefs find it more enjoyable when cooked to 125°F to 130°F/52° to 54°C (medium).

PERFECT SALMON
METHOD 2: USING A CEDAR PLANK

This second method is cooked directly on a wood plank and cooked directly above the hot coals. The smoke coming from the wood plank will permeate the salmon with a nice subtle smoke flavor.

SERVES: 4 « **COOK TIME:** approximately 15–20 minutes

Cedar grilling plank

2 pieces salmon, 1 lb/450 g each

2 tbsp/30 ml olive oil

Salt and pepper

½ tsp fresh dill

6 lemon slices, about ¼"/0.5 cm thick

Set up your grill for two-zone cooking (page 15). Remember that you need a hot side and cool side. You'll be looking for a dome temperature of 375°F to 400°F/191°C to 204°C. Make the proper vent adjustments to obtain the dome temperature. Lump charcoal or briquettes are fine for this recipe.

When grilling with a wood plank, it's not necessary to soak the plank in water. All that does is create steam. What you really want is to place the plank on the grill dry and for it to char and release its nice smoke flavor into the food. The plank will turn black from being directly above the hot coals; the fish will be perfectly cooked.

Place the salmon onto the grilling plank. Drizzle each piece of salmon with about 1 tablespoon/15 ml of olive oil, season with salt, pepper and ¼ teaspoon of fresh dill. Top each piece with 3 lemon slices.

Place the grilling plank with the salmon in the center of the cooking grate. Cook for 15 minutes or until the salmon reaches an internal temperature of 125°F to 130°F/52°C to 54°C (medium). If you like your salmon cooked a little more, then keep it on for another 5 minutes or until you get an internal temperature of 135°F to 140°F/57°C to 60°C.

GRILLED SCALLOPS

More often than not, if you grew up in New England like I did you always had some sort of seafood at least once a week for dinner. For me it was always cod or haddock, then on special occasions we had shrimp. It wasn't until I got into my early teens that I was introduced to scallops. They would always be breaded, then baked in the oven and served with lemon. Then, as I got a little older, I learned you could pan sear them to perfection in only a couple of minutes. I was hooked. Scallops are now my go-to dish when I go out for seafood. With this recipe, I am going to show you how to grill these bad boys perfect each and every time. You won't believe how easy this is!

SERVES: 3–4 « **COOK TIME:** 4–5 minutes

1 lb/450 g scallops

Olive oil

Salt and pepper to taste

Set up your grill for direct cooking (page 11). Remember when spreading the charcoal out in the bottom of the grill, you should have a nice even layer of hot coals. Set your top and bottom vents so you get a dome temperature of approximately 400°F/204°C. Lump charcoal or briquettes are fine for this recipe.

Pat each scallop dry with a paper towel and lay them on a tray. Sprinkle on some olive oil, coating the scallops on all sides. Season the scallops with salt and black pepper. Refrigerate until ready to cook.

Place the scallops on the cooking grate directly over the hot coals and cook for 2 minutes. Carefully check the color; if they have that nice seared color (golden brown), flip them over and cook for another 2 minutes. A perfectly cooked scallop will be seared (caramelized golden brown) on the outside and soft and tender on the inside. An overcooked scallop will be very rubbery, tough and dry (not good eats).

Remove from the grill and serve immediately.

COMPETITION BARBECUE

The basic definition of barbecue is using charcoal to cook meat at a low temperature for a long period of time. In traditional barbecue, the flavor profile consists of a savory spice rub applied to the meat, smoke that slowly seeps into the food during the lengthy cooking time and a sauce that is applied in the final stages of the cooking process.

The Kansas City Barbeque Society (KCBS) sanctions hundreds of contests per year. Each contest has the same four categories: chicken, pork ribs, pork shoulder and beef brisket. I've spent numerous hours learning to cook each category and, drawing from my experience on the competition circuit, I'm going to teach you how to cook all four categories using your Weber kettle grill!

At a barbecue competition, the judges score food according to three core criteria: appearance, taste and tenderness. My culinary knowledge was shaped by learning to cook to these contest criteria, and I quickly realized it was beneficial to keep these benchmarks in mind whenever I prepare food.

For appearance, color is key. The color of the food you're serving should be tantalizing and get people excited to eat. Taste is very subjective, and everyone's palate is different. For the most part, I like to aim for a balanced flavor, where ingredients complement the natural taste of the food. One secret you can keep in mind while cooking is that because everyone's palate is so different, you can always cook with the chef's taste preferences in mind!

Tenderness can be the trickiest of the three criteria, but there are some simple things of which you should be mindful. Generally speaking, perfectly cooked meat should contain moisture and have a nice mouth feel, or texture. Meat that is overcooked tends to be dry or tough, and meat that is undercooked tends to be rubbery or chewy.

The following pages teach how to cook for a KCBS contest. Ready to fire up your Weber kettle grill and cook some barbecue? With just a little practice, it won't be long until you hear your name called up to the winner's circle!

COMPETITION CHICKEN

Chicken can be one of the harder meat categories to master. The skin has to be bite-through, and the meat has to have great flavor. It took a lot of practice, along with some trial and error, but now I have a technique that will improve your chicken results. I like to use chicken thighs. The dark meat has more flavor and will retain its moisture long after it cools.

SERVES: 12 **≪ COOK TIME:** 2 hours and 15 minutes

6 chicken thighs (bone in, skin on)

Simple BBQ Rub (page 120), divided

1 cup/240 ml chicken broth, divided

1–2 chunks apple wood

½ stick of butter/margarine cut into 12 slices

2 disposable aluminum half-pans

Simple BBQ Sauce (page 121) or 1 bottle Smokin' Hoggz Barbecue Sauce

½ cup/120 ml agave or honey

Partially remove the skin from the chicken thighs, but do not remove it all the way. One side will come off very easily, and the other side will still be attached. Lay out the thighs and trim each one into a uniform, trapezoid shape, removing some of the excess fat.

Using a paring knife, scrape the high peaks of excess fat from the back of the chicken skins. With the exposed meat facing up, sprinkle some rub onto the bare chicken and then reattach the skins. (The skin should wrap around the thigh, fully covering the front and about half of the back.) Refrigerate for 4 hours to overnight.

Using a food grade injector, inject about ½ ounce/15 ml of chicken broth into the left and right side of the thighs. Sprinkle the back of each thigh with the barbecue rub and let sit for about 10 minutes to allow the rub to adhere to the chicken.

You should have about ½ cup/120 ml of the injection left over; save this for later on in the cooking.

Using 1 to 2 chunks of apple wood, set up your grill using the C-shape or horseshoe configuration of the snake method (page 13) or the plus-sign method (page 13). You are looking for a temperature of about 250°F to 275°F/121°C to 135°C at the grate level.

Place 6 pads of butter or margarine in each aluminum half-pan. Rest one chicken thigh on top of each pad, skin-side up. Sprinkle the tops of the thighs with barbecue rub. Place the pans on the center of the cooking grate and cook for 1 hour.

After 1 hour, take the leftover injection and add approximately ¼ cup/60 ml to each pan, cover the pan with aluminum foil and continue to cook for 1 hour more.

This process will allow you to get that desired bite-through chicken skin. The liquid in the pan creates steam, which helps tenderize the skin. The internal temperature of the chicken will reach 190°F/88°C, but the chicken will not be overcooked. Because the meat was injected, it will remain juicy.

For this step I like to use a 16-inch/41-cm round, mesh pizza pan. If you don't have one, you can use a cookie cooling rack instead.

(continued)

COMPETITION CHICKEN (CONTINUED)

When the chicken has about 15 minutes remaining, heat the barbecue sauce in a medium saucepan.

Remove the thighs from the grill. Using tongs or gloved hands, submerge each thigh into the warm sauce. Shake off any excess sauce and place the thighs on the cooling rack. Put the cooling rack on the grill, and cook until the sauce is caramelized, approximately 15 minutes.

Spread out a large sheet of aluminum foil. Squirt 12 swirls of agave or honey onto the foil, then sprinkle a pinch of dry rub onto each swirl.

Remove the thighs from the grill. Place each thigh, skin-side up, on an agave swirl. Let rest for 10 minutes and serve.

> **NOTE:** The first competition category is chicken. You can serve white or dark meat chopped, pulled or sliced. My favorite chicken entry is thighs. Thighs contain dark meat, which naturally has more fat than white meat, and helps produce a moist finished product.

Preparing to remove the skin.

Detaching the skin from the meat.

Laying out the skin.

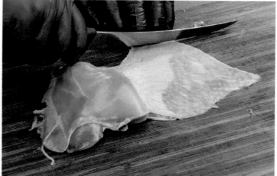
Trimming the skin.

ng the chicken.

Almost done.

Trimming around the top knuckle.

he top is trimmed.

Wrapping the trimmed thigh.

Skin back on the thigh.

d trimmed thigh.

Applying the rub to the backside.

Injecting the thigh.

thigh on a butter pad.

Applying the rub to the top.

Dunking in sauce.

COMPETITION RIBS

Ribs are why I got into this obsession of competition barbecue. I started using St. Louis–style ribs because they are meatier and have a little bit more fat content than the more common baby backs. When cooked right, these spare ribs are so juicy, tender and oh so flavorful. Here is the recipe that has helped us win New England BBQ Society Ribs Team of the Year four years in a row!

SERVES: 8 « **COOK TIME:** approximately 4½ hours

2 racks of St. Louis–cut spareribs

1 cup/240 g Simple BBQ Rub
(page 120)

3–4 chunks of either sugar maple or
apple wood

2 cups/475 ml honey

1½ cups/350 ml Simple BBQ Sauce
(page 121) or 1 bottle Smokin' Hoggz
Barbecue Sauce, divided

1 stick butter, cut into 8 pieces

NOTES: A rib rack holds the ribs upright, so they cook vertically. You can use a rib rack to cook more than two racks of ribs, but keep in mind it will increase your cooking time by about an hour.

The second competition category is pork ribs. When you bite into a perfectly cooked rib, the meat should pull cleanly from the bone. Despite the marketing claims of a particular restaurant chain, a perfectly cooked rib should not fall off the bone. If most of the meat pulls away in one bite, then it's a good sign the rib is overcooked. At best, overcooked rib meat is just expensive pulled pork, at worst it's incredibly mushy and makes for an unpleasant dining experience that lands you lousy scores.

First, trim your ribs according to the photos on page 106. Then lay out the ribs with meat side facing down, apply the rub to the back side of the ribs, and let sit for about 10 minutes. Flip over and apply the rub to the meat side; let the rub sit on the ribs for about 15 minutes, then apply another coating of rub. Let sit for another 30 minutes.

Set up your grill using the C or horseshoe method (page 13). You'll be looking for a temperature of 250°F to 275°F/121°C to 135°C. Set the bottom vent to half and your top vent fully open. Just before placing the ribs on the grill, add the 3 to 4 chunks of sugar maple and/or apple wood.

Place the ribs on the cooking grate and cook for 3 hours.

Lay out 2 sheets of heavy duty foil; apply 2 ounces/60 ml of honey and ¼ cup/60 ml of barbecue sauce; place the ribs, meat side down; now apply 2 ounces/60 ml of honey, ¼ cup/60 ml of barbecue sauce and 4 pieces of butter to the bone side of the ribs and wrap tightly. Repeat process for the other rack of ribs.

Return to the grill and cook for approximately 1 more hour; check the ribs for doneness. To check if ribs are done, look at the back side of the ribs. First, the meat will have shrunk from the bone about ¼ to ½ inch/.5 to 1 cm, and secondly, the bones will start to pop through on the back side.

If the ribs are done, remove them from the foil and place on a flat surface. Now take about ½ cup/120 ml of juices from the foil and ½ cup/120 ml of barbecue sauce and use this as your glaze.

Place the ribs back onto the cooking grate and apply the glaze with a brush. Allow to cook an additional 15 to 30 minutes or until the glaze is tacky to the touch.

Slice the ribs between each bone and serve.

(continued)

Removing the membrane.

Trimming excess fat.

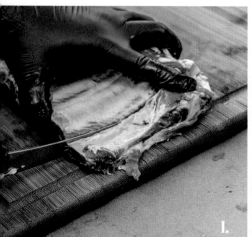

Removing the end bones.

Finished trimming.

ed spare rib.

Applying the rub.

On the grill.

honey on the tin foil.

Pouring sauce on the tin foil.

Pouring honey on the ribs.

sauce and butter to the ribs.

Wrapping in foil.

Ready to return to the grill.

COMPETITION PORK

The meat used in competition pork category comes from the pork shoulder, which is usually divided into two cuts of pork, the shoulder and the butt. Pork shoulder or butt has a very high intramuscular fat content. This fat provides both the challenge of cooking and the reward of eating barbecue pork. The challenge is rendering the fat without overcooking the meat. The reward is a tender, moist, flavorful product that is hard to beat.

YIELD: approximately 6 lbs/2.7 kg of cooked pork **« COOK TIME:** approximately 10–12 hours

1¼ cups/300 ml apple juice or white grape juice, divided

2 tbsp/30 g kosher salt

½ cup/120 ml water

½ cup/110 g brown sugar

1 tsp/5 g cayenne pepper

2 tbsp/30 ml soy sauce

¼ cup/60 ml apple cider vinegar

1 bottle of Stubb's Pork Marinade, strained

Simple BBQ Dry Rub (page 120)

4 chunks of apple and sugar maple (2 each)

1 Boston butt, bone-in, 7–8 lb/3.2–3.6 kg

Yellow mustard (or honey mustard)

1½ cups/350 ml Simple BBQ Sauce (page 121) or Smokin' Hoggz Barbecue Sauce

To make the pork injection, combine 1 cup/240 ml of apple juice, salt, water, brown sugar, cayenne, soy sauce and apple cider vinegar, and stir until the salt and sugar are completely dissolved.

To make the pork braise, mix the Stubb's Pork Marinade, ¼ cup/60 ml of apple juice and 1 tablespoon/15 ml of dry rub, and heat just before using.

Using 4 chunks of apple and sugar maple, set up your grill for using the S or snake method (page 13). You're looking for a temperature of approximately 250°F/121°C. Start with the top and bottom vents completely open, then as you get close to the desired temperature, start to close the bottom vent. You'll end up with the bottom vent about 50 percent closed and the top vent about 25 percent closed.

Trim the pork butt of any extra or loose fat, but keep the fat cap on. This will help protect the butt and help to keep the moisture in. (Remember fat is flavor.)

Using a food grade injector, inject the pork injection, making sure the majority of the injection goes into the muscle opposite the bone (a.k.a. money muscle) and the muscles around the bone. Wipe off any injection on the surface of the butt with a paper towel to get ready for the next step.

Apply a coating of the mustard to the outside of the butt; you don't need too much. All this is doing is making a nice surface for the rub to adhere to. After you coated the butt with mustard, generously apply the dry rub.

(continued)

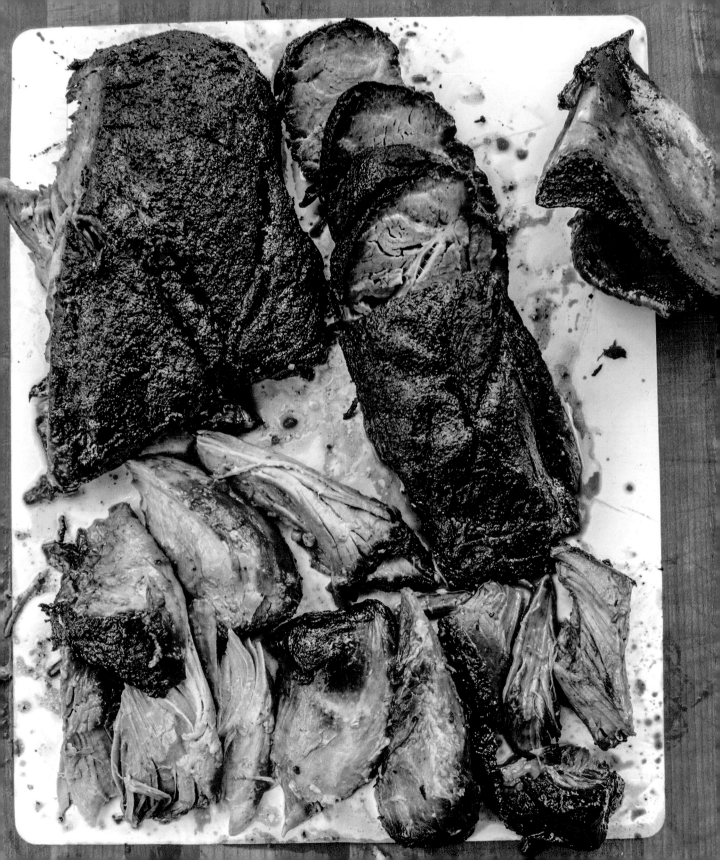

COMPETITION PORK (CONTINUED)

Wrap the butt in plastic wrap and put in the fridge until about an hour before it goes on the grill.

Remove the pork butt from the refrigerator and apply another generous coating of rub. Let sit about 30 minutes before placing on the grill.

Place the butt in the center of the cooking grate, fat side down. Cook until it reaches an internal temperature of about 160°F to 170°F/71°C to 77°C (approximately 6 to 7 hours).

Lay out a sheet of heavy duty foil (big enough to fully wrap the butt). Place the butt fat-side down and pour pork braise onto the butt, completely wrap with foil and return to the grill. Cook until the internal temperature of the muscle opposite the bone reaches approximately 185°F/85°C (approximately 2 to 3 hours). When that temperature is reached, remove from the grill and separate that piece. Glaze with barbecue sauce, wrap in a fresh piece of foil and rest in an insulated cooler or warming box. Rewrap the rest of the butt and return to the grill. Cook to an internal temperature of about 190°F to 195°F/88°C to 91°C or until it probes tender (approximately 2 hours).

Remove the butt from the grill, open the foil and allow the steam to dissipate (approximately 10 minutes). This will help to stop the cooking process. During this time, apply a coating of barbecue sauce to the top surface of the butt. Close the foil and let rest for a minimum of 1 hour; you can use a dry empty cooler lined with some old towels.

> **NOTE:** The third competition category is pork shoulder. You can serve pork chopped, sliced, pulled, chunked or shredded. Properly cooked pork shoulder will be tender and have moisture. Boston butt usually contains a blade bone, and it's my preferred choice for my pork entry. The lower region of the pig's front limb is usually referred to as a picnic shoulder. The picnic shoulder usually contains more skin than the Boston butt. When you slow cook the picnic shoulder, the skin gets nice and crispy, and turns into a flavorful bark. The bark makes for good eating, and every now and again I like to cook a picnic shoulder in the backyard, but for a contest, it's always Boston butt.

(continued)

...ming loose fat off.

Top of pork butt trimmed.

...ming excess fat from bottom. Keep the fat cap on for flavor.

Bottom of butt trimmed.

Injecting into the muscle opposite the bone.

Seasoning.

More seasoning.

Finished butt in foil.

ving the front muscle.

Slicing the front muscle.

slicing.

Pulling chunks.

COMPETITION BRISKET

In my opinion, brisket is the hardest competition category to cook properly on a consistent basis. When perfectly cooked, beef brisket is the juiciest, most tender, flavorful piece of meat your mouth will ever know! There are two cuts of meat associated with a brisket: the flat and the point. The flat is just that, a flat rectangular piece of meat that makes up the majority of the brisket. It's the leaner of the two pieces and is what you will be cutting into slices. The point is the other part of the brisket. It lies across part of the flat and is a fattier piece of meat. You can also slice this section, but it's better for making chopped chunks of meat or for serving up velvety smooth burnt ends.

YIELD: 8–9 lb (3.6–4 kg) cooked brisket « **COOK TIME:** 8–10 hours

4 chunks hickory or oak wood

12–13 lb/5.4–5.9 kg brisket

Brisket Injection (page 122)

Brisket Rub (page 122)

Brisket Marinade (page 123)

Simple BBQ Sauce (page 121) or Smokin' Hoggz Barbecue Sauce

Set up your grill for using the S-shaped configuration of the snake method (page 14). It's at this point you will add the smoke wood to the configuration. You're looking for a temperature of approximately 250°F/121°C. Start with the top and bottom vents completely open, then, as you get close to the desired temperature, start to close the bottom vent. You'll end up with the bottom vent about 50 percent closed and the top vent about 25 percent closed.

Trim all the loose fat and silver skin from the flat side of the brisket. Remove all but ¼ inch/.5 cm of fat from the point.

Next, inject the meat with the brisket injection. Starting at the opposite end from the point, and perpendicular to the grain of the meat. Inject every 2 inches/5 cm going in a checkerboard pattern. Repeat the same thing for the point.

Season the brisket with the rub. Brisket is a very thick piece of meat, and it can handle a lot of rub, so feel free to season generously. Wrap the brisket tightly using plastic wrap, and place it in a fridge or cooler until about an hour before putting it on the grill.

Remove the brisket from the fridge or cooler and touch up any rub that has come off. Light the charcoal, insert the pizza pan or heat sink and then place the brisket in the center of the cooking grate. Cook until you reach an internal temperature of about 160°F to 170°F/71°C to 77°C, approximately 6 to 7 hours.

When the brisket is at the desired temperature, lay out a large piece of heavy duty foil (you want it big enough to wrap the entire brisket). Place the brisket on the foil, fat side down, and add the brisket marinade. Wrap the brisket completely and put back on the grill until you reach an internal temperature of approximately 200°F/93°C or until it probes tender, approximately 2 to 3 hours.

(continued)

COMPETITION BRISKET (CONTINUED)

Remove the brisket from the grill and carefully open the foil. Opening the foil will release steam, which helps stop the cooking process. Let the brisket rest for about 10 minutes.

After the brisket rests, coat its surface with some of the barbecue sauce. Wrap the brisket back up and allow it to continue to rest in a dry empty cooler for a minimum of 1 hour.

Time to make some burnt ends! Take the brisket out of the cooler and carefully unwrap it. Make sure you save as much juice as possible!

Using a large slicing knife, separate the flat from the point by gently cutting along the fat line between the two pieces of meat. If the brisket is cooked properly, there should be little resistance when slicing (like a hot knife going through room-temperature butter).

Wrap the flat back up, and cut the point into 1-inch/2.5-cm cubes. Place the cubes into a disposable half-pan. Add some barbecue sauce, and put the pan onto the grill for an additional 30 to 45 minutes.

While you're waiting for the burnt ends to finish, go ahead and slice the flat. Brisket dries out quickly, so place the slices into the juices you saved. Let the slices continue to sit in the juices until the burnt ends are done.

> **NOTE:** The final competition category is beef brisket. I think it's fair to say that brisket is the most challenging category at any barbecue contest. One thing that makes brisket such a challenge is that it is a very tough piece of meat made up of two muscles, and each can cook at a different rate. You have to develop your skill and be able to determine when each muscle is properly cooked.

...ing the brisket.

More trimming.

...ving the loose fat on top.

Trimming more loose fat.

...ing up the flat.

Removing the fat from the point.

COMPETITION BRISKET (CONTINUED)

Removing more fat from the point.

Trimming fat from the bottom.

Finished trimming.

More injecting.

Injecting.

Seasoning (it can handle a lot).

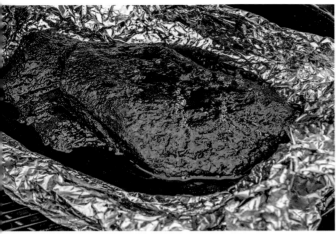

t finished in foil.

Separating the flat and the point.

nue separating.

Separated.

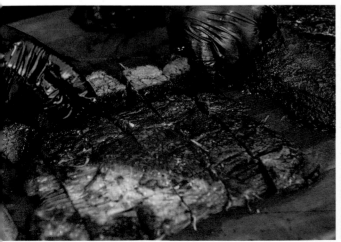

g the point for burnt ends.

Cubes and slices.

SIMPLE BBQ RUB

I think every cook or barbecue enthusiast needs a simple dry rub at their disposal. This rub is just that. This is a great little seasoning for pretty much anything you want to put it on—from seafood to pork shoulder, and anything in between. You can adjust this rub to your liking and desired tastes.

YIELD: approximately 1 cup/240 g « **PREP TIME:** 10 minutes

2 tbsp/25 g organic white sugar

2 tbsp/15 gpaprika

2 tbsp/30 g kosher salt

2 tbsp/30 g firmly packed brown sugar

2 tbsp/15 g garlic powder

1 tbsp/7 g coarse ground black pepper

1 tbsp/8 g onion powder

1 tbsp/8 g chili powder

2 tsp/5 g cumin

1 tsp/2 g oregano

½ tsp cayenne pepper

Mix all the ingredients well and store in an airtight container.

SIMPLE BBQ SAUCE

Here is a simple but tasty barbecue sauce you can easily make at home. There is a good chance that all of the ingredients reside in your cabinets right now. If not, they're certainly available at your local grocery store. One thing I really like about this sauce is how it balances the sweetness of brown sugar and honey with the tartness of vinegar and tomato. At the same time, just a hint of heat from the chili powder cuts through, rounding out the flavor profile. Another thing I like about this sauce is the color. After you make my version of this sauce, feel free to play around with the ingredients and tweak it the next time!

YIELD: approximately 2½ cups/600 ml « **PREP TIME**: 15 minutes

1 package dry onion soup mix (if you have a spice grinder or a food processor, you'll want to grind up the onions from the mix, unless you like a chunky sauce—then keep them as is)

1½ cups/350 ml of ketchup

½ cup/55 g packed brown sugar

2 tbsp/30 ml cider vinegar

¼ cup/60 ml honey

1 tbsp/15 ml molasses

1 tsp/3 g chili powder

Mix all the ingredients well and store in the fridge until ready to use.

BRISKET RUB

Brisket rubs are a little different than most other rubs. Unlike the sweeter chicken and pork rubs, Texas-style brisket rubs traditionally use an equal mix of salt and pepper, sometimes called a Dalmatian rub. This brisket rub adds a savory element as well, which, during the cooking process, translates into a nice exterior coating called bark or crust. Although I created this rub for brisket, sometimes I use it with any kind of beef, like steaks or burgers. Be creative and have some fun!

YIELD: approximately 1½ cups/350 g « **PREP TIME**: approximately 10 minutes

6 tbsp/90 g kosher salt

¼ cup/30 g chili powder

3 tbsp/35 g organic white sugar

3 tbsp/20 g coarse black pepper

1 tbsp/8 g garlic powder

2 tsp/5 g onion powder

2 tsp/4 g oregano

Mix the ingredients well and store in an airtight container until ready to use.

BRISKET INJECTION

Injections and marinades add flavorful liquid to raw meat. Typically, injecting allows the liquid to penetrate more deeply into the meat than marinating. Additionally, because you're adding liquid, the finished product will be more moist and juicy than meat that is not injected.

YIELD: approximately 2 cups/475 ml « **PREP TIME:** 15 minutes

1 tbsp/15 ml beef base (I like this better than bouillon)

2 cups/475 ml high-quality water

½ tsp garlic powder

½ tsp onion powder

1 tbsp/15 ml Worcestershire sauce

Mix all the ingredients well and store in the fridge until ready to use. This should be good in your fridge for about 2 weeks.

BRISKET MARINADE

I call this a marinade but in essence it's really a braising liquid. This is going to add an extra layer of flavor and help make the brisket tender and full of moisture.

YIELD: 1½ cups (350 ml) « **PREP TIME:** 15 minutes

6-oz/180-ml can dark beer

¼ cup/60 ml Worcestershire sauce

6 oz/180 ml water

2 tbsp/30 ml beef broth concentrate (sodium free)

1 tbsp/8 g garlic powder

1 tbsp/8 g onion powder

1 tbsp/15 g brisket rub

1 tsp/3 g cayenne pepper

Mix and heat right before use.

PIZZA

In every neighborhood, it seems like there are people who prefer a particular pizzeria. We all have our personal preferences. That's just part of what makes us human, I guess. While the earliest writings that mention pizza date way back to the tenth century, the flatbread dish we all know and love today appears to be connected to the Naples region of Italy in the eighteenth and nineteenth centuries.

Some people might be surprised to find information about pizza in a grilling book. Don't be; wood-fired brick ovens date back to ancient Rome, and some were unearthed during the archaeological excavations of Pompeii. Charcoal is simply burned wood, and I like how it gives a light smoky flavor to pizza crust. A lot of other people must, too, because there are restaurant chains that market wood-fired pizza. The best part is, once you know the technique, you can have a delicious, fresh-baked pizza from your Weber kettle grill in 10 to 12 minutes—and that's faster than any delivery place I've ever found!

I learned about making pizza on the grill during backyard cooking competitions. There are some excellent third-party kettle grill inserts specifically designed for making pizza, but they're not required. During my early competition days, we didn't have one, but we still scored pretty well in this category. Because you can make pizza in your Weber kettle with or without an insert, this chapter has a recipe for both methods. After you learn the basic cooking process, you'll discover it works for just about any style pizza you want to make, and pretty soon your backyard will be the go-to place for the best pizza in the neighborhood!

BASIC CHEESE PIZZA
FIRST METHOD

Pizza on the grill—yeah, this is a good thing. If I had to choose my favorite style of pizza, it would be a nice thin-crust, New York–style pizza. There are other varieties to choose, from thick Chicago-style deep dish to the Greek style, where the crust is a little lighter and more airy. Pizza is all so tastefully wonderful. It can be pretty hard to make your own dough, so I am fine with buying premade pizza dough—in fact, it's what I usually do. If you have a favorite pizza place, go in and ask to purchase some of their dough. Many places will be happy to sell you some. In this recipe, I'm going to show you two methods of setting up your grill for cooking a delicious pizza. Those fancy-pants coal-fired pizza joints that serve wine won't have anything on what you'll be sharing with guests in your backyard!

SERVES: approximately 2–4 « **COOK TIME:** approximately 10 minutes

1 dough ball for 16"/41-cm pizza

1 cups/240 ml pizza sauce (whatever you like)

2 cups/480 g provolone/mozzarella cheese blend

1 tsp/3 g oregano

Take a full chimney of lump charcoal and spread it out in a circular ring pattern on the lower charcoal grate. Make sure to leave an empty space in the middle of the charcoal ring. If you don't, the crust will not cook evenly and the center will burn, which just isn't good for pizza. You'll be looking for a dome temperature of around 400°F to 450°F/204°C to 232°C. Open the bottom vents to about 50 percent as a starting point. From there you can adjust the vents to obtain the desired temperature. I like to use lump charcoal when making pizza because it burns a little hotter and cleaner than briquettes. You'll get a nice, subtle, smoky flavor from the coals.

Stretch out the dough, forming a circle about 16 inch/41 cm in diameter. With a fork, go around the entire surface of the crust and poke holes; this will help prevent air pockets from forming as the pizza cooks. Place the dough directly onto the cooking grate. The next step is very important: leave the dough on the grill for 1 to 2 minutes. The crust will turn a very light-golden color on the bottom. You just want to firm the crust up for easy handling and putting the toppings on—do not leave it on too long. Once the dough firms up, remove it from the grill. Set the crust's cooked side facing up.

Apply the sauce and cheese and sprinkle with oregano.

Place the pizza back onto the cooking grate; cover and cook for approximately 5 to 7 minutes or until the bottom of the pizza is golden brown.

Remove from the grill, cut into slices and serve right away.

BASIC CHEESE PIZZA
SECOND METHOD WITH PEPPERONI

¼ cup/60 ml corn meal

1 dough ball for 16"/41-cm pizza

1 cups/240 ml pizza sauce (whatever you like)

2 cups/480 g provolone/mozzarella cheese blend

1 tsp/3 g oregano

1 package of pepperoni

The second method uses the KettlePizza accessory. This accessory will turn your grill into a genuine pizza oven. I have the basic package, which comes with the pizza-oven insert and a metal pizza pan. You will also need a pizza stone large enough to fit a 12-inch/30-cm pizza and a wood or metal pizza peel to move the pizza in and out of the grill.

The first step is to build a good fire using a chimney starter. Fill it to the top with lump charcoal and fire it up. When it's ready, dump the hot coals in the back of the grill and assemble your pizza oven. Place the lid on and close the vent on top of the lid; keep the lower vents wide open. You will want to reach a temperature of approximately 700°F/371°C.

Now it's time to make the pizza. Sprinkle some of the corn meal onto the pizza peel. Applying corn meal to the pizza peel will help the pizza slide off onto the pizza stone when putting it into the grill to cook.

Stretch out the pizza dough into roughly a 12-inch/30-cm circle. Place it onto the pizza peel and add your toppings just like in method one, except this time try adding a little pepperoni!

Gently slide the pizza onto the pizza stone and cook for about 2 to 2½ minutes. Rotate the pizza 180 degrees and cook another 2 to 2 ½ minutes. Check and see that the bottom of the crust is a nice golden brown. If not, leave it in for another 1 to 2 minutes, but make sure it doesn't burn.

Here's a little trick if the top of your pizza needs some more time to cook: you can lift the pizza into the upper part of the dome lid with your pizza peel, giving just a little more time to make that cheese nice and bubbly. This is called "doming" your pizza.

Remove the pizza from the grill, cut into slices and serve right away.

RASPBERRY, MASCARPONE AND CHOCOLATE DRIZZLE DESSERT PIZZA

Looking for a different angle for dessert at your next gathering? Try making this dessert pizza. Raspberry, blackberry, sweet mascarpone and chocolate drizzle tie everything together, making this the perfect little after-cookout treat!

SERVES: 4–8 « **COOK TIME:** approximately 5–7 minutes

1½ cups/350 g mascarpone cheese

2 tbsp/30 ml honey

1 store-bought dough ball for 16"/41-cm pizza

1 cup/120 g raspberries

1 cup/145 g blackberries

1 8-oz/230-g jar chocolate sauce, heated

1 8-oz/230-g jar raspberry sauce, heated

¼ cup/30 g confectioners' sugar, for dusting

Mix the mascarpone cheese and the honey together and keep in the fridge until ready to use.

Take a full chimney of lump charcoal, and spread it out in a circular ring pattern on the lower charcoal grate. Make sure to leave an empty space in the middle of the charcoal ring. If you don't, the crust will not cook evenly and the center will burn, which just isn't good for pizza. You'll be looking for a dome temperature of around 500°F/260°C. Open the bottom vents about 50 percent as a starting point. From there you can adjust the vents to obtain the desired temperature. I like to use lump charcoal when making pizza, because it burns a little hotter and cleaner than briquettes. You'll get a nice, subtle, smoky flavor from the coals.

Stretch out the dough, forming a circle about 16 inches/41 cm in diameter. WIth a fork, go around the entire surface of the crust and poke holes; this will help prevent air pockets from forming as the pizza cooks. Place the dough directly onto the cooking grate. The next step is very important: leave the dough on the grill for 1 to 2 minutes. The crust will turn a very light golden color on the bottom. You just want to firm the crust up for easy handling and putting the toppings on—do not leave it on for too long. Once it gets light brown in color, flip it and cook another 1 to 2 minutes.

Remove it from the grill and put on a flat surface. Spread the mascarpone cheese on as a base. Add the raspberries and blackberries. With a spoon (or squeeze bottle), drizzle the heated chocolate sauce across the pizza. Now do the same thing with the heated raspberry sauce, but go in the opposite direction.

Place it back on the grill for 2 minutes just to heat the fruit. Remove it and dust lightly with the confectioners' sugar. Cut into 4, 6, 8 or however many pieces you like, and serve.

> **NOTES:** An easy way to heat up any kind of chocolate- or fruit-based sauce is to place the jar in a pot of simmering hot water. It will make it easier to drizzle the sauce on whatever you are using it for!
>
> If using the KettlePizza accessory, this recipe will make two smaller pizzas.

GRILLED SANDWICHES

Warm, crunchy bread, and gooey, melted cheese make grilled sandwiches something worth getting excited about! One taste of the melded flavors that charcoal brings to sandwiches and you'll want them grilled all year long! You can make any of these grilled sandwich recipes in about fifteen minutes. They're quick, they're easy to make and I'm sure you're already familiar with the sandwiches we'll discuss. Put out a spread of grilled sandwiches the next time your friends gather to watch football and watch what happens.

GRILLED CHICKEN CAPRESE PANINI

Another one of my favorite dishes in the summer is a caprese salad. Fresh basil and heirloom tomatoes, mozzarella cheese and a balsamic reduction. It's so light and refreshing. I thought maybe I could add a little grilled chicken to this and turn it into a sandwich—and even better a grilled panini! Here you go—easy to make and something I am absolutely proud to serve!

SERVES: 2 « **COOK TIME:** 6 minutes

2 grilled chicken breasts (page 47)

8 large basil leaves, divided

¼ cup/60 ml balsamic glaze

4 slices tomato

4 oz/113 g log fresh mozzarella cheese, cut into 4 slices

2 fresh ciabatta rolls

¼ cup/60 ml olive oil

Salt and pepper to taste

Set up your grill for two-zone cooking (page 15). Remember that you need a hot side and cool side. You'll be looking for a dome temperature of 375°F to 400°F/191°C to 204°C. Make the proper vent adjustments to obtain your dome temperature. Either lump charcoal or briquettes are fine for this recipe.

Follow the instructions for cooking the chicken breast, then slice each breast into ½-inch/1-cm slices.

Assemble the sandwich by adding the basil and sliced chicken, then drizzle balsamic over the sliced chicken. Add tomato, mozzarella cheese and more basil. Brush the top and bottom of the roll lightly with olive oil.

Place onto the hot side of the grill. Place weight on top of the sandwich (see note), cover the grill and cook for 3 minutes. Flip, add weight, cover and cook another 3 minutes.

Remove from the grill and serve.

> **NOTE:** To make your own panini press for the grill, take a heavy object—you want something with a flat surface (like a brick)—and wrap it in heavy duty aluminum foil. And there you have it—a simple press for grilling sandwiches.

GRILLED BOLOGNA SANDWICH

I think every kid in America grew up eating bologna and cheese with mayo or yellow mustard on white bread. It was always thinly sliced, the cheese was the American cheese that was individually wrapped and tasted like plastic and the bread would always stick to the roof of your mouth! LOL. Good times! I want to bring this childhood American classic back, but this time bigger and better and cooked on the grill.

SERVES: 2 « **COOK TIME**: 15 minutes

2 slices of bologna, ¾"/2 cm thick (ask your deli person)

2 tbsp/30 g softened butter

2 deli-style sourdough rolls

¼ cup/60 ml brown spicy mustard or mayo (I like mustard)

4 slices American cheese

1 bag potato chips

Set up your grill for two-zone cooking (page 15). Remember that you need a hot side and cool side. You'll be looking for a dome temperature of 375°C to 400°F/191°C to 204°C. Make the proper vent adjustments to obtain your dome temperature. Either lump charcoal or briquettes are fine for this recipe.

Place the slices of bologna on the cooking grate directly over the hot coals and cook until you get some nice grill marks, about 3 to 4 minutes. Flip and cook another 3 minutes. If you want a little smoke flavor with your grilled bologna, add ½ cup/90 g of wood chips directly onto the hot coals while you are grilling it. Apple or peach woods are great, but use what you like!

Spread the softened butter to the cut side of the rolls. Place on the grate over the hot coals and cook until lightly toasted, about 1 to 2 minutes.

Apply mustard or mayo to the top and bottom roll. Starting with the bottom roll, add cheese, a slice of bologna, another piece of cheese and then a few potato chips. Place the top of the roll on and put on the cool side of the grill, just until the cheese starts to melt, about 2 to 3 minutes.

Remove from the grill, serve and think back to your childhood when eating this sandwich!

GIANT BONELESS RIB SANDWICH

We've all had the McRib sandwich; it's basically a bunch of pork pieces pressed together to look like a rack of ribs. Not very appetizing, right? Well, I've got a little something here I am sure you will like—the Giant Boneless Rib Sandwich, made with an actual rack of ribs, without the bones. Yes, you heard right! OK, so when I'm cooking ribs, I like to cook a couple of extra racks (I love ribs heated up on the grill the next day) and put them right into the fridge just so I can make this monster rib sandwich the following day.

SERVES: 4 « **COOK TIME:** approximately 90 minutes

¼ cup/60 ml melted butter, plus more to coat the bread

2 large onions, sliced

Salt and pepper, to taste

1 rack baby back ribs

1 cup/240 ml Simple BBQ Sauce (page 121) or your favorite barbecue sauce, divided

1 large loaf Italian bread

1 tbsp/10 g sesame seeds

In a saucepan over medium heat, melt the butter and add the sliced onions. Stir until the onions have softened and are starting to brown, about 3 to 4 minutes. Season with salt and pepper. Spread the onions in an even layer, cover the pot and reduce heat to low. Stir every 5 or so minutes. Continue until the onions are nice and brown and caramelized—about 25 minutes. This may take longer depending on how many onions you use.

Set up your grill for two-zone cooking (page 15). Remember that you need a hot side and cool side. You'll be looking for a dome temperature of 375°F to 400°F/191°C to 204°C. Make the proper vent adjustments to obtain your dome temperature. Either lump charcoal or briquettes are fine for this recipe.

Place the ribs wrapped in the foil onto the cool side of the grill and cook for about 45 to 60 minutes. The reason for using a leftover rack of ribs is that you have to slightly overcook them to remove the bones, and they will still hold together and not fall apart.

Remove the ribs and let sit for about 5 minutes. Open the foil, grab hold of the first bone and gently twist and pull out. Do this for the rest of them.

Now what I like to do is take a ¼ cup/60 ml of the juices from the foil and a ¼ cup/60 ml of Simple BBQ Sauce, mix together and brush on both sides of the ribs. Then place them back onto the hot side of the grill, cook for 5 minutes, flip and cook another 5 minutes. This is to get a little bit of char from the sugars in the barbecue sauce. Remove from the grill and loosely tent with foil.

Cut the loaf of bread open, brush both sides with butter, sprinkle the top of the bread with sesame seeds and place the bread cut-side down over the hot coals and cook just until you get that nice golden-brown color—about 1 minute.

Remove the bread and lay the rack of ribs on the bottom half; top with grilled onions, drizzle with more Simple BBQ Sauce, cut into 8 pieces, serve and enjoy!

ROAST BEEF AND CARAMELIZED ONION SANDWICH/PANINI

One of my go-to sandwiches when I am on the road is roast beef and Swiss on pumpernickel, toasted with any kind of spicy mustard. It's something about the spice of the mustard and the flavor of the roast beef that really does it for me. When I am at home, I like to kick it up a little by adding some caramelized onions and throwing it on the grill. The sweetness of the onions totally throws it over the top! I think you'll like this one as well!

YIELD: 2 sandwiches **« COOK TIME:** 14–16 minutes

2 tbsp/30 g softened butter, plus more for buttering the bread

2 medium sweet onions

Salt and pepper to taste

4 slices pumpernickel bread

¼ cup/4 g horseradish or whole grain mustard

4 slices Swiss cheese

1 lb/450 g rare, sliced roast beef

2 bricks wrapped in heavy duty aluminum foil

In a saucepan over medium heat, melt the butter and add the sliced onions. Stir until the onions have softened and are starting to brown, about 3 to 4 minutes. Season with salt and pepper. Spread the onions in an even layer, cover the pot and reduce heat to low. Stir every 5 or so minutes. Continue until the onions are nice and brown and caramelized—about 25 minutes. This may take longer depending on how many onions you use.

Set up your grill for two-zone cooking (page 15). Remember that you need a hot side and cool side. You'll be looking for a dome temperature of 375°C to 400°F/191°C to 204°C. Make the proper vent adjustments to obtain your dome temperature. Either lump charcoal or briquettes are fine for this recipe.

Butter only one side of each piece of bread. Spread horseradish or mustard on the other side of the bread.

With the mustard-side facing up, layer with cheese, ¼ of the caramelized onions, ½ pound/230 g roast beef, ¼ of the caramelized onions and a slice of cheese. Place the top piece of bread on.

Place the sandwich on the cooking grate directly over the hot coals; place the brick on top of the sandwich. Close the lid and cook for 2 to 3 minutes. Flip and repeat process for another 2 to 3 minutes.

Move the sandwich to the cool side and continue to cook for 10 minutes.

Remove and serve.

TRUE GRILLED CHEESE SANDWICH

Another classic American comfort-food favorite: the grilled cheese. White bread, American cheese and a piping hot cast-iron skillet. Pair that with a bowl of tomato soup on a cold, rainy day, and there's nothing better. I think that is everyone's childhood memory. I wanted to try a new take on the true American classic by sprucing it up a bit and getting it into the twenty-first century—and it's not as hard as you'd think. Just a really good combo of cheeses and a heartier type of bread—that's all! You'll be amazed at what that can do!

SERVES: 2 « **COOK TIME:** approximately 10 minutes

½–1 cup/60–120 g fresh grated extra-sharp cheddar cheese (if the bread is rectangular you will need the extra cheese)

½–1 cup/60–120 g fresh grated Gruyère cheese (if the bread is rectangular you will need the extra cheese)

½ tsp chili powder

4 slices country or sourdough bread (either one is fine), ½"/1 cm thick

1 stick butter, softened

¼ cup/60 ml Frank's RedHot sauce

Set up your grill for two-zone cooking (page 15). Remember that you need a hot side and cool side. You'll be looking for a dome temperature of 375°F to 400°F/191°C to 204°C. Make the proper vent adjustments to obtain your dome temperature. Either lump charcoal or briquettes are fine for this recipe.

In a bowl, mix the two kinds of cheese and chili powder. Butter the bread on both sides.

Take ¼ of the cheese and spread it evenly on each piece of buttered bread.

Place each piece of bread with cheese on the cooking grate directly over the hot coals, place the lid on and cook for approximately 2 minutes. Be careful at this step, the bread can burn if the coals are too hot. If that's the case, move the bread to the cooler side of the grill.

Combine the two pieces of bread together and place on the cool side of the grill, place the lid and cook for 7 to 8 minutes, until the cheese is fully melted.

Serve with Frank's RedHot on the side for dipping and enjoy!

APPS, SIDES AND VEGGIES

I get bored with vegetables. In fact, I'm not sure I like them very much to begin with. So it's easy to see why I get bored of them. Growing up, vegetables were always boiled. The boiled Irish kind of boiled, and the boiled Irish kind typically lack flavor. When you throw vegetables on the grill and get them to char, now that's a whole different experience. For starters, they're a lot prettier, and everyone likes to eat things that are pretty. The high heat of the grill caramelizes the natural sugars that vegetables contain. This adds a depth of flavor that tastes almost nutty. I think the crunch on grilled vegetables is also a little different. Grilling something as simple as romaine lettuce creates a whole new dining experience.

As you become a better backyard cook, you'll learn to maximize the burn time of your charcoal. Typically, a full charcoal chimney will burn for about 50 minutes. You can roast just about any vegetable or side dish, and many times it takes 15 minutes or less. Sometimes, I like to keep the protein simple, so it doesn't have to be the star of the plate and let the sides do the talking. Cooking up veggies, appetizers or sides can be a lot of fun—just watch what happens when you bring grilled finger food or sides to a family picnic!

GRILLED ONIONS AND PEPPERS

Another staple in my grilling bag of tricks is always having grilled onions and peppers. I think these two veggies are a must-have when grilling because they go with any protein you're cooking on the grill—burgers, steak, pork chops, sausage, chicken, et cetera. Plus, they're quick and easy to grill up.

YIELD: 2–4 servings **« COOK TIME**: 4–6 minutes

2 large sweet onions (I like Vidalia onions)

2 large green bell peppers

¼ cup/60 ml olive oil

Salt and pepper to taste

Fire up your grill for direct cooking (page 11) and make sure you spread out the coals evenly so you don't get any hot spots. Either lump charcoal or briquettes are fine for this recipe

Trim off the ends of the onions and slice into ½-inch/1-cm slices, keeping the slices together. Cut the peppers in half, from top to bottom and remove the stem and seeds. Cut each pepper in half again so you have a total of four pieces from each pepper. Lightly brush the onion and pepper slices with olive oil and season with salt and pepper.

Once the grill is heated up, place the onions and peppers on the cooking grate directly over the hot coals. Cook for 2 to 3 minutes, flip and cook an additional 2 to 3 minutes.

> **NOTE:** If you have the grill grate accessory, this is another great recipe to use it on. Place the grill grate directly on top of the existing cooking grate and let it heat up for 10 to 15 minutes. When heated up, place the onion and pepper slices directly onto the grill grate and cook for 5 minutes. Turn the peppers over with tongs and the onions, carefully, with a metal spatula (so they don't break apart) and cook an additional 5 minutes. Once cooked, serve right away.
>
> Not only is this a great accessory to use for this recipe, it can be used for all the veggie recipes in this book.

ABTS (ATOMIC BUFFALO TURDS)

I didn't know what an ABT was until I started competing in barbecue contests many moons ago. But I quickly learned what they were. They are a jalapeño pepper cut in half, filled with cream cheese, wrapped in bacon, cooked to perfection and brushed with barbecue sauce. You can add other things to them like sausage, pulled pork, brisket, et cetera—the possibilities are endless! Here, I will show you how to make these tasty little treats of heaven so you can make them for your friends and family.

SERVES: 8 « **COOK TIME:** 1½ hours

8 jalapeño peppers

8 oz/230 g cream cheese

1 jar red pepper jelly, 8 oz/230 g

16 slices bacon

Smokin' Hoggz Smokey Apple Wood Dry Rub

2 chunks of apple or sugar maple wood

Smokin' Hoggz Barbecue Sauce (or your favorite barbecue sauce)

Set up your grill for two-zone cooking (page 15). Remember that you need a hot side and cool side. You'll be looking for a dome temperature of 375°F to 400°F/191°C to 204°C. Make the proper vent adjustments to obtain your dome temperature. Either lump charcoal or briquettes are fine for this recipe.

Cut the jalapeños in half and remove the seeds and veins. If you like them spicy, you can leave the veins alone.

Take about ½ ounce/14 g of the cream cheese and spread in each of the cavities of the sliced jalapeños.

Then use about 1 teaspoon/5 ml of pepper jelly and spread on top of the cream cheese layer.

Take one of the slices of bacon and starting from the stem end of the pepper, wrap around in a spiral pattern, making sure the end of the bacon is on the bottom of the pepper. Apply the dry rub on all sides.

Place the peppers on the cool side of the grill, add your wood chunks directly onto the hot coals and cook for 1 hour. Brush each ABT with the barbecue sauce and cook 15 more minutes. Brush again with barbecue sauce and cook for another 15 minutes.

Remove the peppers from the grill, let rest for about 5 to 10 minutes and then serve.

> **NOTE:** Do not use thick-cut bacon for this. The thicker cut bacon makes it difficult to wrap around the pepper, and it doesn't cook as well for this application as the thinner sliced bacon does.

BAKED BEANS AND BROWN BREAD ON THE GRILL

Baked beans and brown bread is an old New England tradition dating back to the colonial days. Brown bread is very dense, made from cornmeal, wheat and rye flour and molasses that is steamed in a can, not baked. This was a traditional Saturday night dinner for me growing up: hot dogs cooked in a cast iron pan, baked beans on the stove top and brown bread heated up in the oven, sliced thick and buttered. Man, I can still taste it now. Sometimes my sister and I would fight for the last piece of brown bread, because the ends were always the best part. Every time I have this dish, it always brings up happy family memories. I am going to keep this tradition going, but this time it's all done on the grill!

SERVES: 4–8 « **COOK TIME:** approximately 1 hour

2 cans B&M Original Baked Beans

½ cup/75 g diced sweet onions

½ cup/55 g brown sugar, firmly packed

1 tsp/3 g dry mustard

¼ cup/60 ml molasses

¼ cup/60 ml ketchup

6 slices bacon

1 chunk apple wood

1 can B&M Brown Bread

1 stick softened butter

Grilled Hot Dogs (page 79), to serve

NOTE: If you need to add more charcoal, you can do so by adding about 10 briquettes directly to the lit coals and wait 10 minutes for them to catch, then you're ready to grill again.

Set up your grill for roasting, using charcoal briquettes (page 12). If you don't have charcoal baskets you can use a regular brick to separate the charcoal on either side. Adjust your bottom vents so the dome temperature reaches approximately 350°F/177°C. Also, you want to make sure that the hinged side of the cooking grate is over the coals to make it easier to add more charcoal, if necessary.

In a large bowl, combine the baked beans, onion, brown sugar, dry mustard, molasses and ketchup and mix well. Pour into a small aluminum pan and top with the bacon.

Place the pan on the cooking grate and on the grill. Add the smoke wood. Cover the grill and cook for 1 hour.

Remove from the grill and stir the beans.

To make the brown bread, remove the bread from the can. You'll need a can opener for this. Remove the top and bottom of the can and gently push the bread out.

Slice the bread into ½ to ¾-inch/1 to 2-cm slices and apply a light coating of butter. After the beans come off the grill, place the buttered slices of bread onto the cooking grate directly over the hot coals for about 1 to 2 minutes.

Remove and serve with the baked beans and grilled hot dogs.

GARY'S STEAK POPPERS

This is a recipe I had in my first book, and I love it so much I just had to put it in this book. It's the perfect appetizer for your next cookout or party. Our friend Gary makes these all the time. Even though they are pretty simple to make, they are always delicious, I personally think it's the pickled jalapeño that makes this dish so amazing—well the bacon helps, too! Everything is better with bacon, right?

SERVES: 12 **« COOK TIME:** 15–20 minutes

1 lb/450 g sirloin tip strips

Lawry's Seasoned Salt

½ tsp pepper

1 tbsp/15 ml olive oil

1 lb/450 g bacon

6 oz/180 g cream cheese

4 oz/113 g sliced pickled jalapeños

Cut the steak into 1-inch/2.5-cm pieces, season with seasoned salt, pepper and olive oil and refrigerate for 1 hour to overnight.

Set up your grill for two-zone cooking (page 15). Either lump charcoal or briquettes are fine for this recipe. Remember that you need a hot side and cool side. You'll be looking for a dome temperature of 375°F to 400°F/191°C to 204°C. Make the proper vent adjustments to reach your desired dome temperature.

Cut each piece of bacon into three pieces. Lay out each piece of bacon and place the steak strip at one end. Apply about 1 teaspoon/5 g of cream cheese, place one or two sliced jalapeños on top of the cream cheese, then roll the bacon around it tightly. Use toothpicks to hold it togther.

You can cook these in about 3 separate batches. Place the poppers on the cooking grate directly over the hot coals, 1 to 2 minutes per side, then remove to the cooler side of the grill and continue to cook indirectly for about 15 minutes. Repeat for the remaining poppers.

GRILLED ROASTED WHOLE CAULIFLOWER

I'm sure like most people, you're not a big fan of cauliflower. It's usually steamed until it's a big pile of mush. Oh boy, do I have a treat for you—cauliflower on the grill! This recipe brings cauliflower to a new level, so that even your kids will want to eat it! It's a little crispy on the outside and tender in the middle!

SERVES: 4 « **COOK TIME:** approximately 60 minutes

1 medium head of cauliflower

¼ cup/60 ml olive oil

Salt and pepper to taste

½ cup/120 ml ranch dressing

Set up your grill for roasting, using charcoal briquettes (page 12). If you don't have charcoal baskets, you can use a regular brick to separate the charcoal on either side. Adjust your bottom vents so the dome temperature reaches approximately 350°F to 375°F/177°C to 191°C. Also, you want to make sure that the hinged side of the cooking grate is over the coals, to make it easier to add more charcoal if necessary.

Prepare the head of cauliflower by removing all of the leaves. Then, with a sharp knife, cut the stem flat, so it doesn't tip over while sitting.

Coat the surface with olive oil. You can use a brush if you have one; if not, just drizzle over and use your hand. Season with salt and pepper.

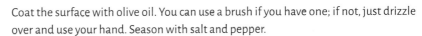

Place the cauliflower in the center of the cooking grate, so that the hot coals are on either side. Cover and cook for about 25 minutes, then start checking for doneness. You are looking for the top to brown nicely and for it to be fork-tender but not mushy. Cook longer if needed.

Break the head up into smaller pieces, toss with ranch dressing and serve immediately.

> **NOTE:** If you like heat, try tossing the cooked cauliflower in buffalo sauce and serving with a side of blue cheese, or try sprinkling some fresh grated parmesan cheese on the top after about 20 minutes of cooking!

GRILLED POTATOES THREE WAYS

GRILLED "BAKED" POTATO

I love potatoes! Growing up, after school to hold me over 'til dinner time, I would make mashed potato sandwiches. Yup, you read that right! Two pieces of white bread on either side of a mound of buttery mashed potatoes! Hence the reason I wore husky-size jeans growing up! Here I'm going to show you how to grill your potato to perfection and serve it three ways!

YIELD: 4 servings **« COOK TIME:** 45–75 minutes (depending on the size of the potatoes)

4 large potatoes

¼ cup/60 ml olive oil

Kosher salt

1 stick butter (8 tbsp/120 g)

Black pepper

Grilled Tomato and Corn Salsa (page 164), optional

Set up your grill for two-zone cooking (page 15). Either lump charcoal or briquettes are fine for this recipe. Remember that you need a hot side and cool side. You'll be looking for a dome temperature of 375°F to 400°F/191°C to 204°C. Make the proper vent adjustments to reach your desired dome temperature.

Wash off the potatoes to remove any dirt or debris. Brush the outside of the potatoes with olive oil, and lightly sprinkle with salt. This will help form a delicious crust when the potatoes are finished cooking.

Place the potatoes on the cool side of the grill and cook for 30 minutes. Rotate the potatoes 180 degrees and cook an additional 30 minutes. Probe the potatoes with a sharp knife; if the knife goes in easily with little resistance, it's done. If not, keep cooking for another 15 minutes, then check again.

When the potatoes are done, remove them from the grill. Slice along the top and spread open. Lather with 2 tablespoons/30 g of butter and a little sprinkle of pepper. Or, if you are looking for something a little different, try topping with grilled salsa.

(continued)

GRILLED POTATOES THREE WAYS (CONTINUED)

GRILLED "MASHED" POTATO

Now I'm going to show you how to make some awesome mashed potatoes from this as well. Follow the cooking directions for the Grilled "Baked" Potato (page 156).

SERVES: 4 « **COOK TIME:** 1 hour

4 large russet potatoes

1 stick butter

½ cup/120 ml heavy cream

2 cloves garlic, minced

1 tsp/1 g fresh chopped parsley

Salt and pepper to taste

Here's what you'll need to do: Cut the cooked potatoes in half and scrape all the potato out of the skin and into a large bowl. Add butter, cream, garlic and parsley. Using a potato masher, mash until smooth. Add salt and pepper to taste. (For an extra-special treat, spread some between two slices of toast, and you'll have one of my favorite childhood snacks!)

GRILLED POTATO WEDGES WITH SPICY KETCHUP

Here's another recipe using the same technique from Grilled "Baked" Potato (page 156).

SERVES: 4 « **COOK TIME:** approximately 60 minutes

1 cup/245 ml ketchup

1 tbsp/8 g chipotle powder

2 tsp/10 ml Worcestershire sauce

4 large russet potatoes

¼ cup/60 ml olive oil

Salt and pepper to taste

To make the spicy ketchup, mix the ketchup, chipotle powder and Worcestershire sauce together and store in an airtight container in the fridge until ready to use.

After cooking the potato for the first 30 minutes, remove from the grill and cut into wedges.

Brush the freshly cut sides of the potato wedges with olive oil and sprinkle with salt and pepper. Place the wedges back on the grill over direct heat and cook for 15 minutes. Flip the wedges and cook an additional 15 minutes. Poke the wedges with a sharp knife. If the knife goes in with no resistance, they are done. If not, cook until done, maybe another 15 minutes. Serve with the spicy ketchup.

GRILLED CORN ON THE COB SERVED TWO WAYS

I love August and September up here in the Northeast! Why? Because that's when all the local corn is harvested and ready to be eaten! We will eat corn two to three times a week during this period, just because it's so good! The corn is supersweet. When grilled and seasoned with a little salt and covered with butter, I'm good for a half-dozen ears! Another way to serve grilled corn is by sassing it up with a bit of chili powder and some Mexican cheese, similar to Mexican street corn. These corn dishes will be sure to wow your friends and family at a cookout!

SERVES: 6 « **COOK TIME:** approximately 17 minutes

6 ears of fresh corn

¼ cup/60 ml olive oil

Salt and pepper to taste

1 stick butter

Set up your grill for two-zone cooking (page 15). Either lump charcoal or briquettes are fine for this recipe. Remember that you need a hot side and cool side. You'll be looking for a dome temperature of 375°F to 400°F/191°C to 204°C. Make the proper vent adjustments to reach your desired dome temperature.

Carefully peel back the husks (but do not completely remove them), so you can discard all the silk. Using butcher's twine or one of the sections of husk, tie the peeled-back husks around the base of the stem. This forms a handle you can use after the corn is cooked and it's eatin' time! Brush the corn with some olive oil and season with salt and pepper.

Place the corn on the cooking grate, directly over the hot coals. Cover and cook for about 3 minutes. Rotate ¼ turn and cook for an additional 3 minutes. Repeat 2 more times, to evenly cook all sides of the ear of corn. Then, move the corn to cool side of the grill and cook for 5 more minutes. Remove the corn from the grill. Roll the corn in some butter and nibble on some Northeast magic.

NOW FOR THAT MEXICAN STREET CORN!

¼ cup/60 ml mayonnaise

¼ cup/60 ml sour cream

½ cup/150 g finely crumbled cotija (if you can't find it, use feta cheese), plus more for serving

½ tsp chili powder, plus more for serving and seasoning

1 medium clove garlic, finely minced (about 1 tsp/5 ml)

¼ cup/60 g finely chopped cilantro leaves

Mix all the ingredients and store in the fridge until ready to use.

Follow the above instructions for cooking the corn. When the corn comes off the grill, transfer to a large bowl and cover with the cheese mixture. Sprinkle with a little extra crumbled cheese and a light dusting of chili powder, then serve.

GRILLED ROMAINE SALAD WITH HONEY BALSAMIC DRESSING

One of my favorite things to eat in the summertime is a grilled romaine salad. The edges of the lettuce get nice and charred, while the center becomes slightly soft yet still has a hint of the crunch that you typically get from a salad. Romaine lettuce contains some natural sugars inside that are released when you grill it. Combine the slightly caramelized greens with something as simple as grated cheese, and the results of this combination are as wonderful as they are crazy!

SERVES: 4 « **COOK TIME**: 3–4 minutes

¾ cup/180 ml olive oil, divided

¼ cup/60 ml good balsamic vinegar

2 tbsp/30 ml honey

½ tsp minced garlic

½ tsp fresh cracked pepper

2 heads romaine lettuce washed and cut in half lengthwise

Salt and pepper to taste

½ cup/90 g freshly grated parmesan cheese

To make the honey balsamic vinaigrette, mix ½ cup/120 ml of olive oil, the vinegar, honey, garlic and cracked pepper together, then store in the fridge until ready to use.

Set up your grill for direct cooking (page 11). Remember, when spreading the charcoal out in the bottom of the grill, you should have a nice even layer of hot coals. Set your top and bottom vents so you get a dome temperature of approximately 400°F/204°C. Lump charcoal or briquettes are fine for this recipe.

Take the 4 halves of romaine and lightly drizzle ¼ cup/60 ml of olive on the cut side. Sprinkle with salt and pepper.

Place the lettuce onto the grill. Grill for 1½ to 2 minutes per side. The lettuce will cook quickly, so you want to check the underside. Watch for a nice char, but don't let the lettuce burn. Flip and repeat for the other side.

Remove the romaine lettuce from the grill and roughly chop into bite-size pieces. Place into a large bowl and toss with the honey balsamic dressing and about half of the parmesan cheese. When incorporated, sprinkle the remaining cheese on the top.

GRILLED TOMATO AND CORN SALSA

I have been making my own salsa for years. It's tastier than the store-bought stuff, plus you can control how hot you want to make it. I thought, hey, I like to grill, why not make a grilled salsa? Well let me tell you, this did not disappoint. The char from the grill brought everything to a whole new level. Rich, smoky, spicy, savory, tangy, yeah it's got it all! This will be the first thing to go at your next cookout, so you better make extra.

SERVES: 4–8 « **COOK TIME**: 15 minutes

1–2 jalapeño peppers, cut in half, seeded, depending on how hot you like it

1 small red onion, cut into ½-inch/ 1-cm-thick slices

6 medium tomatoes, halved

¼ cup/60 ml olive oil, divided

2 garlic cloves, cut in half

2 ears Grilled Corn on the Cob (page 160)

¼ cup/15 g loosely packed fresh cilantro leaves

2 tbsp/30 ml fresh lime juice

Salt and pepper to taste

1 bag tortilla chips

Set up your grill for direct cooking (page 11). Remember, when spreading the charcoal out in the bottom of the grill, you should have a nice even layer of hot coals. Set your top and bottom vents so you get a dome temperature of approximately 400°F to 450°F/204°C to 232°C. Lump charcoal or briquettes are fine for this recipe.

Brush the jalapeño pepper, onion and cut sides of the tomatoes lightly with olive oil. Spray the grilling pan or heavy duty foil with cooking/grilling spray. Place the onion, jalapeño and garlic onto the grilling pan/foil and place that on the cooking grate directly over the hot coals. Cover and cook for 10 to 15 minutes or until golden brown, turning occasionally.

At about the 5 minute mark, add the tomatoes; cover and cook until grill marks appear, turning occasionally.

Remove everything from the grill, and cool for 15 minutes.

Cut the corn kernels from the cobs and discard the cobs. Coarsely chop the onion.

In a food processor, pulse the garlic and cilantro until finely chopped. Add the grilled tomatoes, onion and jalapeño peppers to the food processor, in batches, and pulse each batch until well blended. Transfer to a large bowl. Stir in the corn, lime juice, 2 tablespoons/30 ml of olive oil and salt and pepper to taste. Serve with tortilla chips.

> **NOTES:** If you like chunky salsa, you can dice up all the veggies by hand and then mix together. That's a good option if you want to serve it on tacos or even a baked potato.
>
> A vegetable grill pan is basically a small sheet pan that has small holes all throughout the bottom to allow you to get some nice char on smaller and more sensitive veggies. Also if you don't have a grilling pan/basket, a folded up piece of heavy duty foil with some holes poked through will do the trick.

SUMMER SQUASH AND ZUCCHINI WITH GARLIC OIL AND FETA

One of the things I love about grilling, especially in the summertime, is being able to grill fresh veggies. I'm particularly fond of yellow summer squash and zucchini. I love what the grill does to squash. You get this beautiful caramelization in spots, and the sweet, natural flavors are concentrated, bringing the flavors to another level. I know—you love meat and hate vegetables—but give this a try and veggies won't seem so bad anymore.

SERVES: 2 « **COOK TIME:** 4–6 minutes

6 cloves garlic, roughly diced

1 cup + 2 tbsp (270 ml) olive oil, divided

2 large summer/yellow squash

2 large zucchini squash

Salt and pepper to taste

½ cup/75 g crumbled feta cheese

To make garlic oil, in a small saucepan, bring the garlic and 1 cup/240 ml of oil to a boil. Turn the heat to low and cook for 5 minutes, until the garlic is lightly browned. Turn off the heat and set aside. The garlic will continue to cook. When cool, transfer to a glass jar with a cover. You can store it in the fridge for up to a week.

Set up your grill for direct cooking (page 11). Remember, when spreading the charcoal out in the bottom of the grill, you should have a nice even layer of hot coals. Set your top and bottom vents so you get a dome temperature of approximately 400°F/204°C. Lump charcoal or briquettes are fine for this recipe.

Remove both ends of each squash. Cut in half, lengthwise, to expose the inside. Sometimes the squash come in and they are very large. If that's the case, just cut them into 1-inch/2.5-cm rounds. Brush the insides with the garlic-infused oil and season with salt and pepper.

Once the grill is heated up, place the squash, cut-side down, on the cooking grate, directly over the hot coals. Cook for 2 to 3 minutes. Flip and cook an additional 2 to 3 minutes.

Remove from the grill, cut into bite-size pieces and toss with 2 tablespoons/30 ml of the oil and feta cheese. See, veggies aren't so bad after all.

GRILLED SWEET POTATO

Another one of my favorite veggies is the sweet potato. While it's one of my favorite dishes to have at Thanksgiving, I'm thankful that this is a veggie you can have year-round—especially when grilling during the summer. Grilled sweet potato is wondrous: The inside slowly becomes soft and the natural sugars caramelize. Go ahead and give this a try, I dare you!

SERVES: 2 « **COOK TIME:** 8–10 minutes

2 medium/large sweet potatoes

¼ cup/60 ml olive oil

¼ cup/60 g Smokin' Hoggz Apple Wood BBQ Rub

Set up your grill for direct cooking (page 11). Remember, when spreading the charcoal out in the bottom of the grill, you should have a nice even layer of hot coals. Set your top and bottom vents so you get a dome temperature of approximately 400°F/204°C. Lump charcoal or briquettes are fine for this recipe.

Cut the ends off the sweet potatoes. Using a paring knife or a veggie peeler, remove the outer skin. Slice into ½ to ¾-inch/1 to 2-cm strips, the long way. Brush with oil on both sides and sprinkle with dry rub.

Once the grill is heated up, place the potatoes on the cooking grate directly over the hot coals. Cook for 4 to 5 minutes, flip and continue to cook for an additional 4 to 5 minutes. The potatoes will be done when you can pierce them with a sharp knife and there is no resistance.

Remove from the grill and serve.

FRUIT AND DESSERTS

The perfect way to end a meal cooked in the backyard is with a sweet, decadent dessert. If you've never had a dessert cooked on the grill, you've certainly been missing out! Melted chocolate, salt and crispy bacon—sounds pretty good to begin, right? There is also an abundance of grilled fruit options. Fruit cooks in minutes. When you grill fruit, the flavors morph as the sugars caramelize. To enhance the flavor complexity, consider adding a sprinkle of brown sugar, a drizzle of honey or a pinch of cayenne pepper. Try taking things even further by making a strawberry shortcake right on the grill. The heat from the charcoal will bring a richer flavor to the berries and nuttier taste to the cake. I know you can't wait to get started, so let's turn the page and see what happens next!

BACON WEAVE S'MORES

Move over, graham cracker and say hello to the new kid in town: bacon ! You love bacon, right? Do you love toasted marshmallow? YES! And I know you love chocolate. Put them together and you get pure heavenly bliss. I know you'll want to try this one next time you're at the grill—it will easily become a household favorite.

SERVES: 4 « **COOK TIME:** approximately 30 minutes

2 lb/900 g bacon slices, halved

2 tbsp/25 g brown sugar

2 bars chocolate

16 large marshmallows

4 long skewers or long stick

Set up your grill for two-zone cooking with lump charcoal (page 15). Remember that you need a hot side and cool side. You'll be looking for a dome temperature of 400°F/204°C. Make the proper vent adjustments to reach your desired dome temperature. You want to use lump charcoal here to give the feeling of cooking over a campfire!

To make the bacon weave, lay out three halves of bacon next to each other. Lift one end of the middle bacon slice and place a fourth bacon half on top of the side pieces and underneath the middle slice. Lay the middle slice back down. Next, lift the two side strips of bacon and place a fifth bacon half on top of the middle piece and underneath the sides. Lay the side slices back down. Finally, lift the other end of the middle slice and place a sixth slice on top of the side pieces and underneath the middle slice. Repeat to make seven more mini bacon weaves.

Lay out a sheet of heavy duty foil and lightly coat with cooking spray. Place the mini bacon weaves onto the foil, sprinkle with brown sugar and place on the cool side of the grill, Cover and cook for about 10 to 12 minutes. Check to see if they are browning on top, then rotate and flip the mini bacon weaves, cover and cook for another 10 to 12 minutes.

Move the mini weaves to a paper towel to remove excess grease. Be careful here, as the bacon can stick to the paper towels due to the brown sugar becoming sticky.

Cut the 2 chocolate bars in half and place each half onto one of the mini weaves, Place onto the cool side of the grill to warm up the chocolate.

Put 2 large marshmallows on a skewer and roast lightly over the hot coals, this should only take about 2 minutes, plenty of time for the chocolate to heat up.

Lastly, sandwich the chocolate and marshmallows together with the top bacon weave.

Serve, enjoy and remember you childhood making s'mores over the campfire.

(continued)

BACON WEAVE S'MORES (CONTINUED)

Preparing to make the bacon weave by slicing the bacon in half.

Laying out the base for the weave.

Placing a piece horizontal.

Putting the middle piece over the top horizontal piece to complete the first ro

...ing in the second horizontal piece.

Second row complete.

...ving the third piece to complete the weave.

Completed bacon weave.

GRILLED BANANAS
WITH ICE CREAM AND CARAMEL

This is a very quick and easy dessert that will leave you wondering why you just didn't make more and have only this for dinner!

SERVES: 6 « **COOK TIME:** approximately 3–4 minutes

6 medium, firm, unpeeled bananas

¼ cup/60 ml melted butter

1 tsp/3 g cinnamon, plus more for serving

1 bottle caramel sauce, 8–12 oz/ 180–270 ml

1 pt/350 g vanilla ice cream

Set up your grill for direct cooking (page 11). Either lump charcoal or briquettes are fine for this recipe. Remember to spread the charcoal out evenly to prevent hot spots. You'll be looking for a dome temperature of 400°F/204°C. Make the proper vent adjustments to reach your desired dome temperature.

Slice the bananas in half, the long way, keeping the peel on. Brush the freshly cut side with butter and sprinkle with cinnamon.

Place the bananas on the cooking grate directly over the hot coals cut side down and cook for 3 to 4 minutes, until they are tender.

Remove from grill, gently peel and lay on plate, cut side up.

Drizzle with caramel, add a scoop of vanilla ice cream and lightly sprinkle with more cinnamon.

Enjoy . . . and now you'll know why you wished you made more.

GRILLED FRENCH TOAST

French toast is one of those dishes that can be a decadent breakfast treat, or if you add a little ice cream, it can be a wonderful dessert. I'm going to leave the decision up to you. But what I am going to show you is how to make all your friends and family super envious that you can now make French toast on the grill!

SERVES: 2 « **COOK TIME:** 10 minutes

3 eggs

½ cup/120 ml real maple syrup (not the fake stuff), divided

½ cup/120 ml whole milk

1 tsp/3 g cinnamon

8 oz/230 g mascarpone cheese

6 slices brioche bread, at least 1"/2.5 cm thick

8 oz/240 ml heated caramel sauce

8 oz/240 ml heated chocolate sauce

2 scoops of your favorite vanilla ice cream (optional, use if making it for dessert)

To make the custard mixture, whisk together 3 eggs, ¼ cup/60 ml of syrup, the whole milk and cinnamon until well blended. Keep in the fridge until ready to use.

To make the maple mascarpone cream, combine the mascarpone cheese and ¼ cup/60 ml of syrup; whisk until smooth. Keep in the fridge until ready to use

Set up your grill for two-zone cooking (page 15). Using either lump charcoal or briquettes is fine for this recipe. Remember that you need a hot side and cool side. You'll be looking for a dome temperature of 375 to 400°F/191°C to 204°C. Make the proper vent adjustments to reach your desired dome temperature.

Pour the custard mixture into a 9 x 13–inch/23 x 33–cm baking dish, add the bread and let sit for 1 minute. Then flip the bread and let sit for another 1 to 2 minutes to allow the custard to soak into the bread.

Remove the bread from the custard mixture and place on the cooking grate directly over the hot coals. Cover, with vents towards the cooler side, and cook for 3 to 5 minutes. Start checking for doneness at 3 minutes. If the bottoms are browning up nicely, then flip and do the same for the other side. Move to the cool side of the grill, cover and cook for another 2 minutes.

Remove from the grill and onto a plate, drizzle with maple mascarpone cream, caramel and chocolate sauce, then top with ice cream. Serve and enjoy.

GRILLED PEACHES AND CREAM

Grilled peaches are just awesome. Peaches are sweet and juicy to begin with, and when you add a little grilling action to them, they become heavenly. When you grill them, sugars in the peaches caramelize, which helps create a slightly nutty flavor. Topped with a little crème or Cool Whip and sprinkled with cinnamon, it's heaven on a plate, so get ready to see angels!

SERVES: 6 « **COOK TIME**: 6–8 minutes

6 large peaches, cut in half and pitted

½ cup/120 ml melted butter, divided

¼ cup/55 g brown sugar

½ tsp cinnamon, divided

⅛ tsp ground nutmeg

8 oz/240 ml crème fraîche or Cool Whip

Set up your grill for direct cooking (page 11). Remember, when spreading the charcoal out in the bottom of the grill, you should have a nice even layer of hot coals. Set your top and bottom vents so you get a dome temperature of approximately 400°F to 450°F/204°C to 232°C. Lump charcoal or briquettes are fine for this recipe.

Lightly brush the cut side of the peaches with butter and place on the cooking grate, cut side down, directly over the hot coals. Cook with the lid on for 3 to 4 minutes or until the flesh is caramelized.

Combine the remaining butter with brown sugar, half of the cinnamon and all of the nutmeg. Fill each cavity where the pit was with the mixture, place back on the grill and cook 3 to 4 minutes.

Remove from the grill, place a dollop of crème fraîche or Cool Whip on top, lightly dust with cinnamon and serve. See those angels flutter about? Don't say I didn't warn you!

> **NOTE:** You can also use nectarines, yellow or white, as well as apricots.

GRILLED PINEAPPLE SLICES

One of my favorite fruits to grill is pineapple. Not only does grilled pineapple work as a dessert, it also pairs well with chicken and pork. I love how the natural sugars caramelize to give it an even more intense flavor. You won't believe how easy this recipe is and will probably be wondering why you haven't done this sooner.

SERVES: 4 « **COOK TIME:** approximately 4–6 minutes

1 pineapple, peeled, cored and cut into 1"/2.5-cm slices

¼ cup/60 ml melted butter

1 tbsp/7 g cinnamon

Set up your grill for direct cooking (page 11). Remember, when spreading the charcoal out in the bottom of the grill, you should have a nice even layer of hot coals. Set your top and bottom vents so you get a dome temperature of approximately 400°F to 450°F/204°C to 232°C. Lump charcoal or briquettes are fine for this recipe.

Brush each of the pineapple slices with melted butter and sprinkle with cinnamon; do this to both sides.

When the grill is ready, place the sliced pineapple on the cooking grate directly over the hot coals and cook for 2 to 3 minutes. Flip the slices over and continue cooking for an additional 2 to 3 minutes.

Remove from the grill and serve immediately.

GRILLED STRAWBERRY SHORTCAKE

Strawberry shortcake is a very iconic summertime dessert. Almost every summertime cookout I've gone to, there has been some form of this wonderful dessert and, quite honestly, I am glad, because it's one of my favorites. Traditionally this dessert is made with shortcake, hence the name. However, you can make it with biscuits, sponge cake and, lastly, pound cake, which is how I am going to show you how to make it. I am going to grill the strawberries in this recipe along with the pound cake. When you grill strawberries, the natural sugars in them heat and start to caramelize, which give them a richer flavor, and the pound cake gives off this beautiful toasty, nutty flavor! Let's get to it.

SERVES: 4 « **COOK TIME:** approximately 10 minutes

1 store-bought pound cake

¼ cup/60 ml melted butter

1 lb/450 g large strawberries

1 jar strawberry topping, 8 oz/240 ml

1 container Cool Whip (not the light crap), 16 oz/450 g

Set up your grill for direct cooking (page 11). Remember, when spreading the charcoal out in the bottom of the grill, you should have a nice even layer of hot coals. Set your top and bottom vents so you get a dome temperature of approximately 400°F to 450°F/204°C to 232°C. Lump charcoal or briquettes are fine for this recipe.

Slice the pound cake into eight ½-inch/1-cm slices. With a brush, coat both sides of the sliced pound cake with the melted butter.

Place the whole strawberries on the cooking grate directly over the hot coals, cover and cook for 3 to 4 minutes; flip, cover and cook an additional 3 minutes.

Remove, cut in half and place into a bowl; add about 4 ounces/120 ml of the strawberry topping, mix well and set aside.

Place the pound cake onto the cooking grate directly over the hot coals and cook for 30 seconds to 1 minute or until you see grill marks; flip and do the same for the other side.

Remove the pound cake. Spread some of the whipped topping onto one of the slices. Add strawberries and more whipped topping and place another slice of pound cake on top.

GRILLED LEMONADE

Who remembers as a kid having a lemonade stand? I certainly do! This recipe brings me back to when I was young, and we made real lemonade from real lemons, not from a powder. As I mentioned earlier in this book, one of the things a lot of people enjoy about cooking in the backyard is that they get to play with fire. Another part of the enjoyment factor is that many people play with fire while consuming alcohol. Now, I'm not suggesting that you mix the two; I'm just acknowledging that sometimes it happens. Besides, what's a summer barbecue without a little adult beverage? After all, you have to do something while you're waiting for the meat to cook. Enjoy my absolute favorite one, and drink responsibly!

SERVES: 4–6 « **COOK TIME:** 5–10 minutes

10 lemons cut in half

1¼ cups/250 g sugar plus ½ cup/100 g for dusting lemon halves

2¼ cups/535 ml water for making simple syrup

¼ cup/60 ml fresh mint, loosely packed

1 gallon-size/4-L pitcher

4 cups/950 ml water

4 cups/870 g ice

Burbon, optional

Set up your grill for direct cooking (page 11). Remember, when spreading the charcoal out in the bottom of the grill, you should have a nice even layer of hot coals. Set your top and bottom vents so you get a dome temperature of approximately 400°F to 450°F/ 204°C to 232°C. Lump charcoal or briquettes are fine for this recipe.

Dip each of the halved lemons into ½ cup/100 g sugar to coat.

Place each lemon half onto the cooking grate directly over the hot coals. Cook for about 5 to 10 minutes; check after 5 minutes to see if they are caramelized but not burned. Cook longer if needed.

While the lemons are cooking, bring 2¼ cups/535 ml water to a boil and add the remaining sugar and mint; stir until all the sugar is dissolved, remove from the heat and let sit for about 30 minutes. Strain the syrup and hold until ready to use.

When the lemons are done, remove them from the grill. Squeeze the juice from the lemons into a pitcher. Use a lemon squeezer if you have one; if not, use your hands and try to get as much juice as you can. Add 4 cups/950 ml water, the mint-infused simple syrup and a couple of the grilled lemons. Add ice, stir and enjoy.

If you want to kick things up a little, try adding a bit of bourbon, about 1 ounce/30 ml of bourbon to 8 ounces/226 ml of lemonade, to that freshly made lemonade, sit back, relax and enjoy a nice adult cocktail.

ABOUT THE AUTHORS

BILL GILLESPIE

Bill Gillespie is the founder and head pitmaster for the world champion Smokin' Hoggz BBQ Team and author of *Secrets to Smoking*. Bill spends his days working for the local utility company as a design engineer, but his true passion is grilling and cooking barbecue. For over twenty-five years, Bill has been perfecting his craft in barbecue cooking in his backyard for friends and family. In 2005, Bill joined the barbecue circuit and in 2008 formed Smokin' Hoggz BBQ. Since then, he has gone on to win multiple grand championships and numerous awards including New England BBQ Society Team of the Year in 2014 and 2015, the 2011 Jack Daniel's World BBQ Championship, and the 2014 American Royal Invitational World Series of BBQ, two of the most prestigious BBQ competitions on the circuit. He is also the author of *Secrets to Smoking on the Weber Smokey Mountain Cooker and Other Smokers: An Independent Guide with Master Recipes from a BBQ Champion* and *The Smoking Bacon & Hog Cookbook: The Whole Pig and Nothing but the Pig BBQ Recipes*.

TIM O'KEEFE

Tim O'Keefe has lifetime membership in the Kansas City Barbecue Society (KCBS) and has been active in competition barbecue for over a decade. Based out of the Boston area, his love of barbecue once inspired a 6,000-mile road trip to Lockhart, Texas, just to eat brisket! A certified barbecue judge, Tim has judged over 40 contests sanctioned by KCBS and has been part of the Can U Smell My Pits competition team since 2015. Tim has contributed articles for *National Barbecue News* and *All About Jazz*, and has cowritten three cookbooks with Bill Gillespie.

ACKNOWLEDGMENTS

My wife, Shaune Gillespie, for putting up with me while writing my third book, giving me inspiration when needed and always keeping me grounded and humble. My rock!

My in-laws, Jeanne and Paul Connolly, for spending the entire weekend with us and helping keep things clean and in order.

My teammate and right-hand man (sometimes left) Alan Burke, for helping with the recipe prep and running out every time we needed or forgot something at the store.

Tim O'Keefe for helping me write another book, taking all my thoughts and ideas and turning them into something that people can read and understand.

Ken Goodman for his incredible vision in food photography and always making the food look so amazing.

To my publisher, Will Kiester, my editor, Marissa Giambelluca, and the entire staff at Page Street Publishing for giving me the opportunity to write another book.

Jared and Suzanne Huizenga for taking time out of their busy schedule to help out with the photo shoot.

To all my barbecue friends for their continued support in my barbecue quest.

INDEX